The **Essential** Buyer's Guide

COBRA
REPLICAS

1980 to 2011

Your marque expert:
Iain Ayre

VELOCE PUBLISHING
THE PUBLISHER OF FINE AUTOMOTIVE BOOKS

Also in the Essential Buyer's Guide Series from Veloce Publishing:

Alfa Romeo Giulia GT Coupé (Booker)
Alfa Romeo Giulia Spider (Booker)
Audi TT (Davies)
Austin Seven (Barker)
Big Healeys (Trummel)
BMW E21 3 Series (1975-1983) (Cook & Reverente)
BMW E30 3 Series (1981 to 1994) (Hosier)
BMW GS (Henshaw)
BMW X5 (Saunders)
BSA 350 & 500 Unit Construction Singles (Henshaw)
BSA 500 & 650 Twins (Henshaw)
BSA Bantam (Henshaw)
Citroën 2CV (Paxton)
Citroën ID & DS (Heilig)
Cobra Replicas (Ayre)
Corvette C2 Sting Ray 1963-1967 (Falconer)
Choosing, Using & Maintaining Your Electric Bicycle (Henshaw)
Ducati Bevel Twins (Falloon)
Ducati Desmodue Twins (Falloon)
Ducati Desmoquattro Twins – 851, 888, 916, 996, 998, ST4 1988 to 2004 (Falloon)
Fiat 500 & 600 (Bobbitt)
Ford Capri (Paxton)
Ford Escort Mk1 & Mk2 (Williamson)
Ford Mustang – First Generation 1964 to 1973 (Cook)
Ford Mustang – Fifth generation/S197 (Cook)
Ford RS Cosworth Sierra & Escort (Williamson)
Harley-Davidson Big Twins (Henshaw)
Hinckley Triumph triples & fours 750, 900, 955, 1000, 1050, 1200 – 1991-2009 (Henshaw)
Honda CBR FireBlade (Henshaw)
Honda CBR600 Hurricane (Henshaw)
Honda SOHC Fours 1969-1984 (Henshaw)
Jaguar E-Type 3.8 & 4.2-litre (Crespin)
Jaguar E-type V12 5.3-litre (Crespin)
Jaguar Mark 1 & 2 (All models including Daimler 2.5-litre V8) 1955 to 1969 (Thorley)
Jaguar S-Type – 1999 to 2007 (Thorley)
Jaguar X-Type – 2001 to 2009 (Thorley)
Jaguar XJ-S (Crespin)
Jaguar XJ6, XJ8 & XJR (Thorley)
Jaguar XK 120, 140 & 150 (Thorley)
Jaguar XK8 & XKR (1996-2005) (Thorley)
Jaguar/Daimler XJ 1994-2003 (Crespin)
Jaguar/Daimler XJ40 (Crespin)
Jaguar/Daimler XJ6, XJ12 & Sovereign (Crespin)
Kawasaki Z1 & Z900 (Orritt)
Land Rover Series I, II & IIA (Thurman)
Land Rover Series III (Thurman)
Lotus Seven replicas & Caterham 7: 1973-2013 (Hawkins)
Mazda MX-5 Miata (Mk1 1989-97 & Mk2 98-2001) (Crook)
Mazda RX-8 All models 2003 to 2012 (Parish)
Mercedes Benz Pagoda 230SL, 250SL & 280SL roadsters & coupès (Bass)
Mercedes-Benz 280-560SL & SLC (Bass)
Mercedes-Benz SL R129 Series (Parish)
Mercedes-Benz W124 – All models 1984-1997 (Zoporowski)
MG Midget & A-H Sprite (Horler)
MG TD, TF & TF1500 (Jones)
MGA 1955-1962 (Crosier)
MGB & MGB GT (Williams)
MGF & MG TF (Hawkins)
Mini (Paxton)
Morris Minor & 1000 (Newell)
Moto Guzzi 2-valve big twins (Falloon)
New Mini (Collins)
Norton Commando (Henshaw)
Peugeot 205 GTI (Blackburn)
Porsche 911 (964) (Streather)
Porsche 911 (993) (Streather)
Porsche 911 (996) (Streather)
Porsche 911 (997) Model years 2004 to 2009 (Streather)
Porsche 911 (997) Second generation models 2009 to 2012 (Streather)
Porsche 911 Carrera 3.2 (Streather)
Porsche 911 SC (Streather)
Porsche 924 – All models 1976 to 1988 (Hodgkins)
Porsche 928 (Hemmings)
Porsche 930 Turbo & 911 (930) Turbo (Streather)
Porsche 944 (Higgins)
Porsche 986 Boxster (Streather)
Porsche 987 Boxster & Cayman (Streather)
Rolls-Royce Silver Shadow & Bentley T-Series (Bobbitt)
Royal Enfield Bullet (Henshaw)
Subaru Impreza (Hobbs)
Sunbeam Alpine (Barker)
Triumph 350 & 500 Twins (Henshaw)
Triumph Bonneville (Henshaw)
Triumph Herald & Vitesse (Davies)
Triumph Spitfire & GT6 (Baugues)
Triumph Stag (Mort)
Triumph Thunderbird, Trophy & Tiger (Henshaw)
Triumph TR6 (Williams)
Triumph TR7 & TR8 (Williams)
Velocette 350 & 500 Singles (Henshaw)
Vespa Scooters – Classic 2-stroke models 1960-2008 (Paxton)
Volvo 700/900 Series (Beavis)
VW Beetle (Cservenka & Copping)
VW Bus (Cservenka & Copping)
VW Golf GTI (Cservenka & Copping)

For post publication news, updates and amendments relating to this book please visit www.veloce.co.uk/books/V4395

www.veloce.co.uk

First published in September 2011. Reprinted April 2016 by Veloce Publishing Limited, Veloce House, Parkway Farm Business Park, Middle Farm Way, Poundbury, Dorchester DT1 3AR, England. Fax 01305 268864 / e-mail info@veloce.co.uk / web www.veloce.co.uk or www.velocebooks.com. ISBN: 978-1-845843-95-3 UPC: 6-36847-04395-7.
© 2011 & 2016 Iain Ayre and Veloce Publishing. All rights reserved. With the exception of quoting brief passages for the purpose of review, no part of this publication may be recorded, reproduced or transmitted by any means, including photocopying, without the written permission of Veloce Publishing Ltd. Throughout this book logos, model names and designations, etc, have been used for the purposes of identification, illustration and decoration. Such names are the property of the trademark holder as this is not an official publication. Readers with ideas for automotive books, or books on other transport or related hobby subjects, are invited to write to the editorial director of Veloce Publishing at the above address. British Library Cataloguing in Publication Data – A catalogue record for this book is available from the British Library. Typesetting, design and page make-up all by Veloce Publishing Ltd on Apple Mac. Printed and Bound by CPI Group (UK) Ltd, Croydon, CR0 4YY.

Introduction
– the purpose of this book

Cobra replicas are essentially very fast, bespoke, cottage-industry sports cars. They have jig-welded tubular steel chassis frames in a variety of designs, and fibreglass bodywork originally moulded from a real Cobra and still resembling a Cobra, with some variations. This structure is immensely strong, almost corrosion proof, and will last longer than you will. The lowest budget British chassis (Pilgrim) passed European TÜV strength tests ten years ago, and a more substantial one (Viper) once destroyed a Land Rover in a head-on crash and only required some bodywork repair, replacement Jaguar suspension parts on one side, and an upper wishbone mounting replaced before going back on the road.

A scruffy but genuine Cobra displays character and charm. Sadly, at ●x250,000, they aren't very affordable.

For reference, this is a real Cobra interior – usefully simple and cheap to replicate.

A real AC 427 Cobra is not a thoroughbred racehorse: it's more like a cart horse on crack. The round-tube ladder chassis and flexible aluminium body of the exquisite AC Ace design were fine for a 1919-designed, 2-litre straight six driving on crossply tyres – sublime, in fact – but a 7-litre big-block AC Cobra is grossly overpowered for its chassis, and is a bit of an animal.

I have seen one driven well at Lydden circuit in England, and it was educational. The driver was silky smooth and kept the car balanced on the same throttle and steering settings on the corners, then let rip progressively on the straights, braking only in a straight line. The Cobra rewarded his elegant driving by not spitting him off the circuit into the kitty litter.

A big-block replica is also hard work to drive, although the chassis and body are likely to be much stiffer and more stable than the real thing. Back off on engine weight by choosing a small-block 289/302 Ford V8 or a Rover V8, and you still get potentially dangerous power – but you also get better-balanced weight distribution, mostly good manners, sharp handling, and lighter, more responsive controls.

Cobra replicas are virtually all over-powered and over-braked. The equation is very simple – when you build a donor-based Cobra replica, you throw away a heavy, fully glazed production car monocoque made from folded sheet steel. You replace it with a tubular steel frame inside a small plastic bucket. The resulting car weighs 50 per cent less, and therefore the performance is immediately doubled.

The brakes supplied with the donor car are now also twice as effective and twice as likely to lock up the tyres. There is no electronic stability control and usually no ABS. Cobra replicas will bite anybody who does not treat them with respect and fear: if you panic-brake halfway round a fast corner, you will hit whatever you were looking at before the car started spinning.

The deeper and wider the central tunnel, the stiffer the chassis. Sheet metal adds major stiffness, too.

This applies to even an old Ford-based Pilgrim Sumo with 2-litre Pinto power: even with the donor engine it's still faster than a turbocharged Cosworth Sierra. The danger is only *potential* danger, though – learn the car, know your limits, and cruise safely and happily into the sunset.

Okay, now you know what you're getting into.

Replicas vary widely in style and price. You can buy an extremely accurate aluminium-bodied car made in Poland by Kirkham Engineering and marketed by Hawk in the UK, and by Kirkham and Shelby in the USA, which optionally duplicates even some authentic original minor design mistakes. You can have a visually accurate mid-range replica with a much improved but entirely inauthentic chassis, such as GD's TVR-style backbone. You can buy the cheapest available kit designed to recycle a single scrapped donor car and use your own labour to build a new budget Cobra replica for ●x12,000. You can go off-piste and use the timeless AC Ace/Cobra body shape and any of a dozen wildly different chassis options to build a very personal car – a V12 cruiser (preferably with power steering), an electric runabout, a dragster, a scary turbo propane street/track beast, the world is your oyster.

While British Cobra replicas often reflect limited budgets by recycling components, American Cobra replicas generally don't – they tend to use billet suspension and all-new parts throughout, with the exception of the Mustang-based Factory Five and a few others.

If you don't like attracting attention, don't buy a Cobra replica. Most of the attention you get is admiring, but vegetarian feminists generally won't be impressed.

Do you really want one? Tell you what, just admiring those sublime curves and proportions on a daily basis is payback enough, and trying to achieve decent lap times without spins on a circuit track day will leave a grin on your face that takes days to wear off.

Oh yes, you want one.

Contents

Introduction
– the purpose of this book 3

1 Is it the right car for you?
– marriage guidance 7

2 Cost considerations
– affordable, or a money pit? 11

3 Living with a Cobra replica
– will you get along together? 13

4 Relative values
– which model for you? 15

5 Before you view
– be well informed 17

6 Inspection equipment
– these items will really help 20

7 Fifteen minute evaluation
– walk away or stay? 21

8 Key points
– where to look for problems 23

9 Serious evaluation
– 60 minutes for years of enjoyment 26

10 Auctions
– sold! Another way to buy your dream 39

11 Paperwork
– correct documentation is essential! 42

12 What's it worth?
– let your head rule your heart 45

13 Do you want to build or buy?
– building will take longer and cost more than you think 48

14 Paint problems
– bad complexion, including dimples, pimples and bubbles 51

15 Problems due to lack of use
– just like their owners, Cobra replicas need exercise! 53

16 The Community
– key people, organisations & companies in the Cobra replica world 55

17 Vital statistics
– essential data at your fingertips 58

Index 64

The Essential Buyer's Guide™ currency
At the time of publication a BG unit of currency "●" equals approximately £1.00/US$1.43/Euro 1.28. Please adjust to suit current exchange rates using Sterling as the base currency.

1 Is it the right car for you?
– marriage guidance

Left: Dax is one of the earliest names involved with Cobra replicas. Before 1980 Dax was selling GRP bodies through *Exchange & Mart*. This superb example was recently built by *Kitcar*'s Nigel Dean (www.nigeldean.co.uk)

Tall & short drivers
The space inside a Cobra replica cockpit depends on the individual replica design, some being roomier than others. It's often possible to have the footbox extended if you've found an otherwise ideal car and are ordering a new kit. Don't even think about buying a Cobra replica without trying it on. All Cobras have small doors and require a certain level of fitness to scramble inside, and all are a challenge to enter with the soft top erected.

Weight of controls
Variable according to engine size and position, steering and pedal geometry, and components. Big-blocks and V12s have concrete steering, 289s are better, and all-aluminium Rover V8s are usually nicely light on the steering.

Clutch operation depends on pedal length, master cylinder and slave cylinder bore sizes, and smooth cable runs for cable clutches. All of these can be modified in pursuit of lighter clutch action. As a rule of thumb, gear-changes on massive big-block manual gearboxes are agricultural, and the lighter and smaller the engine, the lighter the gearbox and its action.

The author's Cobretti Viper V8, built in the 1990s and reluctantly sold during a recession. Grrr.

Will it fit the garage?
A Cobra replica won't be too long, but it might be too wide for a standard British garage. Americans don't usually have to worry about that. However, even if you can't open the car's doors inside the garage, you can still scramble over the side, and most Cobra replicas are light enough to be pushed in and out of a tight garage by hand. Maximum length with bumpers will be about 13ft (400cm) and maximum width, 6ft (180cm).

The inauthentic Chevy 350 V8 beats the Ford hands down: bigger, stronger, more powerful, cheaper, and with endless bargain performance options.

The deeper and wider the central tunnel, the stiffer the chassis. Sheet metal adds major stiffness, too.

Interior space

Very comfy for two, once you're ensconced. The driving position is reclined and relaxed, and if the seats are good (check for enough thigh support) you can cruise for hours. Other than an optional glovebox, there's usually no luggage space in the cockpit.

Luggage capacity

Sometimes surprisingly good, depending on where the fuel tank is, and on the design of the boot's interior panelling and floor. The usual 427 body type is very wide indeed at the back, so a well-designed Cobra boot can be enormous. Carry a tyre inflation can, not a spare donor wheel. (Where would you put the deflated but still enormous 235/50 x 17 wheel and tyre you just took off?)

Running costs

A big-block Ford V8 with a rude cam and two 750cfm Holley carbs will get 6mpg (30l/km) and a turbo Mazda four will achieve 45mpg+ (5l/km). (An imperial gallon is 1.2 US gallons.) Other engines will be in-between. A 3.5-litre Rover V8 on SU carbs or injection offers quite good economy, and a 5-speed small-block isn't too bad. American and Japanese components are reliable, and US parts are also very cheap. A four-cylinder Cobra replica could be run for the same money as an MGB, and it won't need new floors and sills as regular service items.

Cobra replicas nearly all use double-skinned GRP doors, boot and bonnet; strong and light. My own door pictured here weighs just 4kg.

Usability

If you keep to a reasonable engine capacity and take advantage of the usefully big boot, the main limitations are having only two seats, and some weather ingress as the soft top design is fairly primitive. Optional detachable hardtops improve this.

The author's prototype body is an improvement on an older American replica, with a lightweight chassis concept beneath it.

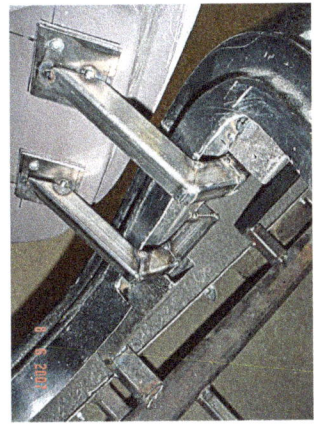

This roughed-in door hinge design is the sort of engineering you see in Cobra replicas: massively over-engineered, but reassuringly over-strong as well.

Parts availability
Donor parts: Cortinas and Sierras are almost gone. BMWs are very cheap and widely available, so they are now becoming a popular budget donor. Jaguar XJ6 running gear availability is okay at the moment, but the supply will inevitably decline. US V8 parts, no problem. Rover V8 parts, okay for the moment. Mazda, again ubiquitous and cheap. Old Mustangs of the right period for a Factory Five will still be okay for a while in North America, not so good elsewhere.

Service and replacement parts: look at the availability of your donor's service parts and think ten years ahead. Obsolescence is speeding up: Ford will be discarding Sierra and Mustang parts, Jaguar XJ6 axle spares will also eventually dry up. On the bright side, new 3.9-litre Rover blocks are now being cast again, and the US aftermarket V8 parts industry is in good health with a long view. Before investing in a kit, look at the Cobra manufacturer's business history, factory expenses and likely survival through this and the next depression.

Repair parts costs
American mechanical parts, very cheap indeed. Ford parts, not too bad. Mazda, quite expensive. BMW, unjustifiably expensive, but you can always scrap another donor.

Insurance
Insurance is surprisingly affordable, as Cobra drivers are a good risk. In the UK, get quotes from MSM, Hagerty, Adrian Flux, Footman James and others advertising in the kitcar magazines. Worldwide, consult local clubs to find a good broker.

No carb means no need for a bonnet scoop on the new Ayrspeed car, so it's reversed and used to extract underbonnet heat generated by the turbo.

Investment potential

Cobras depreciate very slowly, if at all. You won't lose money if you buy a good V8 Cobra replica. The better-regarded marques will hold prices more. However, a profit is unlikely unless you buy and complete an abandoned project, which is an excellent idea, anyway.

The AC Ace represents 1950-1965, ladder-chassis replicas represent 1970-2010, and lightweight turbo Mazda donor rolling gear and carbon bodies take us forward from 2011.

Failings

Wet knees; you get laughed at by jealous people in boring cars if you break down; sidepipes give you headaches and burnt legs; Cobras attract a lot of attention whether you like it or not ... and they're dangerously fast.

Plus points

Huge fun; young ladies sometimes like to stroke Cobra bodywork; Vee-format engines make a viscerally exciting noise; no rust; immense strength ... and they're dangerously fast.

Hawk's 289 replica is basically a V8 MGB with a new, stronger chassis, and a body that will never rust. The cockpit is as inviting as the concept. Who wouldn't want one?

The UK's A-roads might be congested and bristling with tax cameras, but France's Routes Nationales are not. Cobra paradise.

2 Cost considerations
– affordable, or a money pit?

Purchase
The best value to be found in the Cobra replica world is an abandoned project. Quite a few people get to 80 per cent of the build and either lose interest in it or are threatened with divorce, and their misfortune can be your bargain: even if the kit is incomplete, major savings can be made.
Building your own car from a new kit will cost ●x12-50,000 depending on the quality of the kit and components, which will be reflected in its ultimate value.

The minimum price for a functional budget Cobra replica such as a Pilgrim Sumo with a Pinto or V6 Ford engine and box is going to be about ●x12,000. Anything with a Rover V8 will start at around ●x15,000, and a car with Jaguar axles and an American V8 will start at between ●x15-20,000 rising to ●x30,000 for branded performance goodies and leather. American Cobra replicas with custom suspension and serious power run from ●x30-50,000.

The value of a genuine 289 AC Cobra with racing history is counted in houses rather than in pounds or dollars.

Affordable to run?
Once achieved, a top class Cobra replica with rebuilt Jaguar axles, running a good American engine with decent cooling will never stress any of its components. Other than petrol, oil, tax and insurance, there should be virtually no running costs.

At the budget end of the spectrum, a blown-up BMW or Ford engine or axle can be replaced in a weekend for pocket money at the scrapyard.

Buy the best?

Buying the best is not necessary. Only with inside knowledge can you differentiate a well-built Sumo from a well-built Superformance. If your budget is ●x15,000, just enjoy a ●x15,000 Cobra replica. Cheaper ones don't deteriorate any more than expensive ones. Once initiated, you can upgrade if you feel the need. In the UK, if you know nothing about cars, buy from a specialist dealer advertising in *Kitcar* magazine: the car will cost more, but there will be additional security.

Servicing/parts costs

These depend on brand. American V8 rebuild parts costs are almost free: a piston for a 350 Chevrolet V8 can be bought for the price of a pizza. Cobra replicas are also about half the weight of production cars, which is why they're at least twice as fast: components are thus only 50 per cent stressed. Wear of shocks, engines and so on is very slow, given correct lubrication and regular engine oil changes.

Some sample costs: a damaged oil cooler radiator might cost ●x100, a replacement adjustable shock absorber about ●x100, a new electric fan ●x40, a clutch master cylinder ●x30, and a fuel pump ●x25. None of these items carry any huge branded car-dealer profits, so they're sold by Europa or Factory Five on a competitive cost-plus basis. Main dealers don't get their hands on your wallet.

A downside is that many mechanics and garages will be unable to cope with an unusual car for which there is no repair manual. A list of the exact sources of your car's components will be useful.

The author's second Cobra replica was a Ford Cortina-based four-cylinder, bought for very little money indeed. With a Rover V8 and white stripes, it became much more desirable.

3 Living with a Cobra replica
– will you get along together?

Good points
Every time you go anywhere in a Cobra replica, it's an adventure. Their engines don't just start, they fire up. If the engine is a V8 with suitably inadequate silencing, it explodes into life. The power-to-weight ratio is double that of the donor car, even with a relatively feeble standard engine. Once you add serious V8 power and torque, the performance quadruples the power-to-weight ratio, with massive potential acceleration. You can't use too much of it, what with speed cameras in the UK and traffic cops everywhere else, but there is pleasure in effortless muscle: if you want to overtake somebody, just press the throttle firmly, the scenery blurs and you're gone.

For touring, particularly in France and North America where there's a bit of room, a long-legged V8 on Routes Nationales and rural US highways is sublime. It's effortless, there's blipping and growling on corners and roundabouts, and there's acres of room in the boot for luggage and madam's Manolo Blahnik collection. That same capacious boot is useful for supermarket action.

Cobra replica bodies and chassis are all very strong, and you may appreciate this if the worst should happen.

This seat looks weird, but you can bet it will be both comfy and help save the driver from serious injury if rear-ended.

The hugely fat rear end of a 427 replica means that if the kit is well designed, luggage capacity in the boot can be enormous.

A suitable American V8 will normally come with a big four-barrel carb. If you can restrain your throttle foot to just using the first two barrels, fuel consumption can be fairly reasonable.

13

The simplicity of the car will make it inherently reliable and easy to fix in the event of a mechanical issue, and although the noise and firm suspension can be tiring, it's just physical tiredness rather than stress exhaustion – amusing cars reduce stress rather than generate it.

Nearly all men will be envious, but they will get out of your way on the road in order to hear your exhausts. Women respond to Cobra replicas either with annoyance or speculation, and many enjoy riding in hugely expensive-looking cars with fat bums because it makes them look both slim and rich.

There are two UK options for aftermarket Le Mans-style long hardtops, which make a Cobra replica a practical year-round option.

Bad points

You can't avoid attracting attention, and are likely to annoy neighbours with unnecessary rolling thunder. You (and all passengers) will burn your leg on the sidepipes, but just once. You'll get sick of bending your right leg double in order to squeeze into the cockpit. You'll get bored messing about constructing the roof frame and putting the roof up, and you'll get sick of the little waterfall that dribbles round the side of the windscreen and pours all over your knee when it rains. Of course, if you live in California it generally doesn't – one more reason to drive a Cobra replica there.

Most Cobra replicas carry a folding soft top and frame and sidescreens in the boot, which take ten minutes or so to erect. Not exactly waterproof, but better than nothing.

4 Relative values
– which model for you?

Sexy performance badges add a lot of value to a Cobra replica. Roush is a fashionable American performance outfit, so that ticks the box.

Build or buy?
Apart from buying abandoned projects, specification affects pricing more than the build/buy choice. You can either buy, or build, to a price you set.

Budget Cobra replicas
Pilgrim dominates the UK entry-level market, and Factory Five rules in the US, although its budget is higher. ●x12,000 plus a dead BMW (or Mustang) and a few hundred hours' work/play in building it will get a Pilgrim Sumo on the road. A similar figure will buy a previously built secondhand V6 or four-cylinder Pilgrim, or possibly a Rover V8-powered example. Abandoned projects come up worldwide for just a few thousand, with box after box of brand new components.

Original-style round-tube chassis drainpipes, inboard suspension, billet wishbones, no cheap donor bits on view: this is a Cutting Edge kit, a high-quality American replica.

15

Mid-market Cobra replicas

Quite a few Pilgrims have been built to a good standard with V8s, and they trade at the ●x15,000+ level. They also cost about that to build. Most starter body/chassis kits begin at ●x4000-6000, so you can also build a higher-rank car for a fairly similar amount. It's always worth opting for Jag suspension and a V8, as it adds significantly to the value.

This is a top class interior. Leather, woodrim Moto-Lita steering wheel, stainless steel and polished aluminium detailing. (Courtesy Nigel Dean)

Upmarket Cobra replicas

Upmarket cars normally have either Jaguar XJ6 or bespoke suspension, almost invariably an American V8, and leather inside. ●x20,000+ is the level you're looking at here, for a Hawk, a GD, a Dax with more advanced suspension, a well-finished Cobretti, AK or Crendon. In the US and Canada, ●x20,000 tends to be the base price, with high-spec cars rising to ●x50,000.

This turbocharged four-cylinder Mazda engine has scary performance, but is not a V8, which will knock thousands off the value for mainstream Cobra enthusiasts.

5 Before you view
– be well informed

If you know the car is a GD replica, you already have a pretty good idea of what it is and whether it will suit you.

To avoid a wasted journey and the disappointment of finding that a car does not match your expectations, be clear about what questions you want to ask before you pick up the telephone. Some of these points might appear basic, but when you're excited about the prospect of buying your dream car, it's amazing how some of the most obvious things slip the mind. Also check the kit car magazines for current values of the model you are interested in. Some Cobra clubs have cars for sale, such as www.bccobraclub.org

IVA status
In the UK, correct IVA test status is important. Some cars are still passing MoTs with incorrect registrations – people used to change their documents to say 'Cortina Convertible' or some such, but with no new chassis number issued. Increasing computerisation means those cars may eventually be forced to pass an IVA test, which they may expensively fail due to tightened design rules – some of them absurd, but all of them unavoidable. Engine date can be important for emissions requirements: post-1991 means a catalytic converter is required.

In the rest of the world, apart from France, once a registration has been achieved it's usually permanent. Check with kitcar enthusiasts local to you for your own situation.

Where is the car?

You may not find a Cobra replica close to you, as there may only be a few for sale in a particular country or area in any one month. Look at any within reach, even if they seem unsuitable, in order to learn more.

Dealer or private sale?

There are only a few kit car dealers. They advertise in *Kitcar* and sometimes in other magazines. A private owner should have all the history, so don't be afraid to ask detailed questions. A dealer may have more limited knowledge of a car's history, but should have some documentation. A dealer may offer a warranty/guarantee (ask for a printed copy) and finance. Turnkey cars and secondhand cars can often be bought from manufacturers.

Cost of collection and delivery

A dealer may well be used to quoting for delivery by car transporter. A private owner may agree to meet you halfway, but only agree to this after you have seen the car at the vendor's address to validate the documents.

View – when and where?

Always view at the vendor's home or business premises. In the case of a private sale, the car's documentation should tally with the vendor's name and address. Arrange to view only in daylight, and avoid a wet day. Most cars look better in poor light or when wet. Sadly, car fraud is common in the UK.

Reason for sale?

Do make it one of the first questions. Why is the car being sold, and more importantly, how long has it been with the current owner? How many previous owners are there? If there are many, why is that?

Condition (body/chassis/interior/mechanicals)?

Ask for an honest appraisal of the car's condition over the phone, to save wasting everyone's time. Ask specifically about some of the check items described in chapter 7.

Matching data/legal ownership

Do VIN/chassis, engine numbers and number plate match the registration document? Is the owner's name and address recorded correctly?
    For those countries that require an

Ten minutes' research on the telephone will save much time by establishing whether or not an advertised Cobra replica is going to be worth a trip.

annual test of roadworthiness, does the car have a current document (an MoT certificate in the UK, which can be verified on 0845 600 5977)? If a smog/emissions certificate is mandatory, does the car have one? If required, does the car carry a current road fund licence/licence plate tag? Does the vendor own the car outright? Money might be owed to a finance company or bank: the car (or its engine) could even be stolen. Several organisations will supply data on ownership, based on the car's licence plate number or VIN number, for a fee. Such companies can often also tell you whether the car has been 'written-off' by an insurance company. In the UK these organisations can supply vehicle data:
   HPI – 01722 422 422
   AA – 0870 600 0836
   DVLA – 0870 240 0010
   RAC – 0870 533 3660
   Other countries will have similar organisations.

Unleaded fuel
If necessary, has the car been modified to run on unleaded fuel? Engines from before the mid-1970s may have issues.

Insurance
Check with your existing insurer before setting out, as your current policy might not cover you to drive the car if you do purchase it.

How you can pay
A cheque/check will take several days to clear, and the seller may prefer to sell to a cash buyer. A wad of waved fifties is very tempting to a seller. A banker's draft (a cheque issued by a bank) is theoretically as good as cash – invite the seller to accompany you to your bank when collecting it, to reassure them it's a real one. There are fake banker's drafts about, so while it's safer to pay with one than to carry cash, it's less safe to accept one as payment.

Buying at auction?
If the intention is to buy at auction, see chapter 10 for further advice. Cobra replicas tend not to come up at auction very often.

Professional vehicle check (mechanical examination)
For production cars, there are often marque/model specialists who will undertake professional examination of a vehicle on your behalf. However, Cobra replicas are too unusual for many of these. The owners' clubs are key – the owners know the cars inside out, and are happy to help out prospective new club members. Taking a car for an MoT as part of your test drive is also well worthwhile. If the owner refuses, don't buy the car.

The smaller Cobra manufacturers may be able to identify and discuss individual cars they have made from a description of the car.

6 Inspection equipment
– these items will really help

This book
Before you rush out of the door, gather together a few items that will help as you work your way around the car. This book is designed to be your guide at every step, so take it along and use the check boxes to help you assess each area of the car you're interested in. Let the seller see you using it.

Reading glasses (if you need them for close work)
Take your reading glasses if you need them to read documents and make close-up inspections.

Torch or flashlight
A torch or flashlight with fresh batteries will be useful for peering into the wheelarches and under the car.

Probe (a small screwdriver works very well)
A small screwdriver can be used – with care – as a probe, just in case there is any chassis rust, although this is very unlikely.

Overalls
Be prepared to get dirty. Take along a pair of overalls, if you have some.

Mirror on a stick
Fixing a mirror at an angle on the end of a stick may seem odd, but you'll probably need it to check the condition of the underside, pipework etc. It will also help you to peer into some of the important crevices.

Digital camera
If you have the use of a digital camera or even a phone camera, take it along so that you can study some areas of the car more closely later. Take a picture of any part of the car that raises concerns, and seek knowledgeable opinions.

A sensible friend, ideally from the Cobra Club
Ideally, have an experienced friend or enthusiast accompany you. Joining the Cobra Replica Club will yield many such friends.

A disappointed expression
The disappointed facial expression is a useful buying tool: even if you're gagging to buy the car, express visible and audible doubts about its value and desirability when beating down the price.

7 Fifteen minute evaluation
– walk away or stay?

Paperwork
The right paperwork is critically important in the UK: if the car is not registered absolutely correctly, it could finish up as an undrivable ornament next time you take it for an MoT test. It is possible to get an older kit car through the ●x500 current government testing, but there are many expensive and sometimes absurd hoops through which you have to jump. If the car has a period number plate, check that it is registered as a product of the kit manufacturer with a new chassis number, and not as something like a 'Jaguar Sports' with the original VIN. If it has a 'Q' plate it's already registered as a collection of assorted parts so it will be okay. If it has a recent registration it should have passed whatever version of the SVA/IVA/BIVA government test is current. A check to see if it's stolen is also wise.

In most of the USA, the registration and testing regime is simple, but emissions can be an issue in some states. In California, 500 kitcars a year are allowed to be registered and emissions-tested based on the model year they resemble, ie 1965 for Cobra replicas. Apply early ...

If this car were for sale, 15 minutes would establish that it is a good quality brand, a V8, good paint and colour, and of tidy construction.

Exterior, bodywork
Cobras are expected to be metallic blue with white stripes, and anything else will tend to lower their value in the public's eye. Ferraris are supposed to be red, Cobras blue. Fibreglass bodywork can be tricky to paint well, so check for micro-blisters, fisheyes, bubbles, chips, and an absolute smoothness of line along the main body panels. Some Cobra replicas are surprisingly ripply, either because of mould imperfections or engine-heat-related sagging and shape changes. The word 'plastic' means malleable, and Cobra bodies are plastic.

Look inside panels for messy fibreglass layup and stray untrimmed bits of matting and resin. The next buyer will knock money off, so you should as well.

Many panels on GRP bodies are difficult to fit well, so back off a few paces and just look at the bonnet, boot and doors – are they symmetrical? Do they fit in their apertures properly?

If you see evidence of cracking at one end of the car, it may be referred damage from an impact at the other end – GRP can transfer shocks in strange ways. Unlike a steel monocoque, properly repaired damage on a chassis-based GRP car is nothing to worry about, but it needs checking and it lowers the car's value.

Check underneath for visible chassis damage, and, if anything worries you, measure diagonally across the frame to check straightness. Bear in mind that it may not have been made quite straight when new and that it may not matter: these are handmade cars. If anything worries you, talk to the manufacturer, walk away, or deduct the cost of a replacement chassis, which could be as low as ●x2000.

Build quality
Look at the brake and fuel lines and their securing clips in the engine bay and under the car. This section of the build is a boring and time-consuming task, and it can be carried out in two ways – impatiently, by someone who's rushing to finish the car, or detailed and perfect, with smooth piping bends and equidistant 6in spaced clips, by an anal-retentive, picky engineer type. Do the pipes and clips say the build is sloppy and careless? If you're not prepared to rebuild such a car to get it done properly, walk away. If you do want to rebuild it, make an insultingly low offer that reflects the 300 hours of work you'll have to do.

Interior
There isn't really much interior involved in a Cobra. Cobretti's leather interior kit, comprising seats, door panels, dashboard leather, glovebox and back panel, costs ●x1150. If a leather interior is worn or damaged, this is the sort of money it will cost to replace it. Alternatively, you can update with a huge variety of new seats from Europa or other *Kitcar* magazine advertisers, starting from ●x200 per pair.

The unforgiving interior colour also indicates that the car is either almost new or fastidiously looked after. Well worth a full examination.

Gearbox
An autobox shifter rather than a manual gear lever is bad news for the car's value, although privately I'll tell you that an American autobox with a ratchet shifter makes the car faster off the line and more pleasant to drive.

The choice of manual gearbox must also match the engine. A high-performance 350 Chevy on a Supra gearbox, unless it has turbo-spec bearings, will not handle being hammered on for long, although with a standard 350 and reasonable use it can work fine and provides a nice light gearchange. A Rover V8 with a Rover gearbox in good condition is okay, and a Rover V8 mated to a Ford Sierra gearbox is okay if the Rover engine remains fairly standard. A T5 will work well with a 302 Ford engine. A big-block American V8 needs a big and agricultural gearbox – you want to hear words like Muncie, Saginaw, top-loader ...

Engine
Look under the bonnet: if you don't see a V8 you might want to walk away, unless you're saving more than ●x5000. Nearly everybody wants a blue/white 427 replica with a V8. A V6 or a Pinto or BMW engine means a poverty Cobra, but as long as you buy at the right price, you can always put in a Rover engine later. You can't replace a Pinto with a 350 Chevy engine without upgrading earlier Ford axles and the brakes as well, but you can retrofit a standard Rover V8 to replace a Pinto or V6, to bring the car up to reasonable respectability.

8 Key points
– where to look for problems

Check body and paint for flaws and ill-fitting panels. Doors and other opening panels can be badly fitted, even on upmarket replicas, so check all round the gaps.

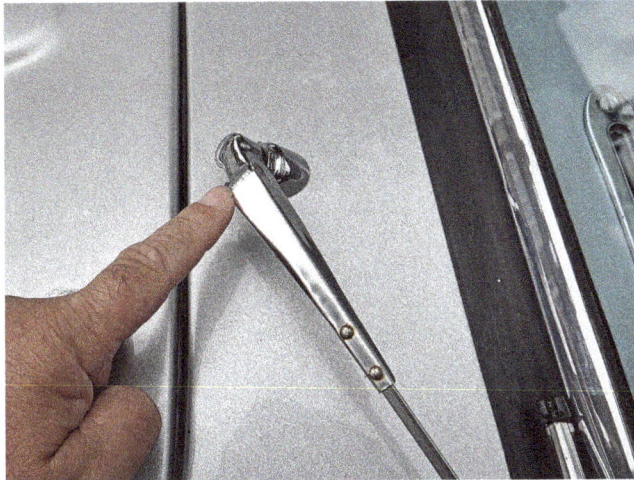

Wiper mechanisms are tricky to fit well, as their correct geometry is not always obvious. Check that operation is smooth, and that the washer system works properly.

Wheels and tyres can suffer cuts and kerbing damage on the inside as well as the outside, and even perfect-looking tyres can be well past their safe age limit.

Lighting and other wiring faults are relatively inexpensive to sort out (frequently just a ground/earth problem), but problems reduce the buying price you'll offer.

Check the operation and accuracy of all the dashboard instruments. Check the speedo against a GPS. Minor and consistent inaccuracy we can live with – but at a reduced price.

US gear changing can be hard work, with a brutal clutch. Check for gearbox noise, jumping out of gear – is the gearbox type up to the task? (Sierra box is okay for mild Rover, not for Chevrolet.)

Check the interior for function as well as condition: do the seat rails slide and lock well? Are the seatbelts chafed or damaged, and do the door catches work correctly?

Listen to the engine on cold start-up. Check oil condition and compression. Check cooling system for emulsion, condition, size, shrouding, and auto fan operation with the bonnet shut.

Check for noises and leaks from the differential, and either ensure that it's strong enough for the engine type, or lower your offer, and budget for keeping a couple of spares.

Check the exhaust for secure mountings, leaks, and excessive noise, which is a UK MoT fail. Underfloor systems are expensive, but in my opinion offer a big improvement.

Suspension and steering bushes and bearings can wear, shocks can leak; check for the proper fasteners. Bad suspension adjustment or design can result in heavy steering and a brutal ride.

Brakes should be checked for fluid leaks, hose condition and warped discs. Do they pull evenly? Does the back lock up first? Handbrake okay (particularly important with inboard XJ6 rear discs)?

9 Serious evaluation
– 60 minutes for years of enjoyment

Score each section using the boxes as follows:
4 = excellent; 3 = good; 2 = average; 1 = poor. The totting up procedure is detailed at the end of the chapter. Be realistic in your marking!

This Viper V8 was for sale at the time of writing, for about ●x15,000. It's very old for a Cobra replica, but age is irrelevant. The body is GRP, the chassis is massive, and it's been well looked after.

Viewing and inspecting a Cobra replica is quite different from checking out a classic production car, in which you're peeking into nooks and crannies looking for corrosion, wear and bodges that have occurred over decades and a hundred thousand miles. A Cobra replica is essentially a very strong steel frame covered up with a plastic bucket, usually with minimal sunny-day-only mileage, so many of the normal secondhand car examination rules don't apply.

Some do, however, and there are plenty of other pitfalls.

Avoid DIY amputations
Don't take any risks when examining a car. In particular, don't rely on a jack to hold it up. Don't ever put anything you want to use again under a jacked-up car, such as your arm or your head. Get the car up on a pair of ramps, wheels chocked and in gear, or supported on axle stands, before getting under it.

Exterior
Any baggy old disaster of a car looks fab at night and in the rain, so that's when you don't buy one. Always look at a car in daylight, and if possible, back it into a garage, crouch down and look along the body sides towards the light – any peculiarities will reveal themselves. A weird but effective way of examining a car is to hand-wash it: the seller will be puzzled but is unlikely to turn down the offer. Your hands quite often pick up anomalies, and during the process you will naturally examine every inch of the bodywork with your eyes as well as your fingers.

Bodywork symmetry and fit is variable in Cobra replicas. There was once a real Cobra from which moulds were taken, but most replica bodies are copied from earlier kit bodies made from generations of moulds – sometimes changed and improved, sometimes changed and not improved. The original price of the kit isn't always a good guide, as some cheap Cobras have nice symmetrical bodywork, while some expensive ones need a little work. If there are ripples and bumps and the panels don't fit very well, knock the price down or move on and find a better-shaped car if the visual details really bother you. The feel and character of the whole car is probably more important than the precision of the shell shape: once you've looked at a few Cobra replicas you'll know what your priorities are.

GPP bodywork is very strong, but look inside panels for cracks – sometimes damage inflicted on one corner can reappear as referred damage elsewhere on

This Viper's interior is in red leather, just beginning to be worn in, and nowhere near worn out. The same applies to the Rover engine with its four Dell 'Orto carbs.

the body. If it needs repairs, carrying them out is quite easy, but damage obviously reduces the value.

The finish of the invisible inner surfaces can be cheap, rough and careless – that's an area that varies a lot car-by-car. Structurally, it doesn't matter, so it's up to you how important you feel it is.

Old steel production cars can be piles of dangerously corroded scrap, beautifully and expertly reconstructed with newspaper and body filler. This doesn't apply to Cobra replicas: the chassis are massively thick and strong, and the bodywork does not deteriorate with time – a 1950s kitcar special body could have sat in a field for sixty years and still be structurally as good as new. In any case, GRP body damage is easy to restore to its original strength and finish.

With Cobra replicas, what you see is, rather refreshingly, what you get.

Reason for sale

The condition and specifications of the car are much more important than what somebody tells you about why they're selling it, but if the car is dodgy and being moved on for bad reasons, you might smell a rat by probing a little. If you gaze thoughtfully at people and keep quiet, they will quite often start babbling and tell you much more than they wanted to.

One aspect of Cobra replicas is that a surprisingly large number of people simply love building kit cars but can't be bothered with driving them; they regard the whole thing as a jigsaw puzzle, and lose interest as soon as it's finished.

Another aspect is that getting V8s to stay cool in a small engine bay can be a pain, and getting the cars to ride well can take some time, so the seller may have been disappointed and just decided to get rid. Some people just go sour on the whole long and expensive building process, and find that the fun has gone out of it. Yet more have put a finished Cobra up for sale because they were scared of it.

Legalities and the registration minefield

There are complications with British kit cars in that the paperwork and testing has suffered from a major Elf'n'Safety attack during the last few years, inspired by EU 'harmonization.' I was involved at the very beginning of the SVA test design, when German TÜV engineers came over and advised British civil servants to look for safe design, safe brakes, safe handling and working lights. This somehow got twisted into a test that demanded rolled edges on exhaust tailpipes to avoid pedestrians risking being cut while being run over by reversing kitcars, and other such nonsense, which obscured the useful parts of the test and bred contempt and resentment. It also costs nearly ●x500, which is just another tax.

If you're building a new kit, most manufacturers are up to speed with the test requirements, and it's really no more than an expensive nuisance. Even if you buy an old kit that was designed long before testing, having to go through the test is not a serious problem, although passing IVA will add dramatically to the car's value. Old kits often have headlamp heights set too low, and upper seatbelt mounts set too low. For old Cobra kits, you simply use adjustable-height coilover shocks, and jack the car up until the headlights are legal. For seatbelts, you use retractable lap-and-diagonals the wrong way round, and put the upper location on the highest point of the tonneau panel behind the seats, or hook them on to a roll-over bar. Those are pretty much the worst that can happen. The prospect of the test will scare many people off, though, so knock a very big chunk off your offer if there is any risk of having to go through it.

This car isn't for sale, but let's evaluate it as if it were. Body and paint are good, but we don't actually know what brand it is ...

Cars with period registrations and a new chassis number are fine. Of my own kit cars, the first was based on a J-registered tax-free 1971 Triumph Vitesse and is now a Triumph Midge, re-registered with a new SAB TVRO chassis number. The next was a K-registered tax-free 1972 Jaguar XJ6-donor Chevy-powered Cobretti Viper V8, the third was a tax-free 1972 K-registered Jag-based Ayrspeed Six (an XK120 replica), and the second Cobra replica was a Q-registered Viper 4 constructed with parts from no identified year, which paid road tax. The free-tax loophole is now apparently closed. All of my cars were correctly registered according to contemporary rules, so I never had a problem.

Cars that have passed SVA and IVA will have new registrations or newly-issued period registrations, and recently amateur-built cars should have a set of build photographs with them – get those or copies of them to keep with the car's paperwork. A car that has passed SVA or IVA is probably going to be worth more than one that has never needed to pass it, as the test is comprehensive and reassuring for anybody new to kit cars. I suspect that a good few new production cars would fail it.

Other than the test complications, you need to check that the name and address of the owner tallies with that on the registration document, and you need to see those documents and the car at that address. There are many thieves and conmen operating in the British secondhand car market, and buying a dodgy Cobra replica would be an expensive mistake.

An HPI check is also wise, as a significant percentage of secondhand British cars have something nasty in their past. It would be upsetting to buy a Cobra replica and then find out that it still belonged to somebody else.

Different rules apply worldwide and in different states and provinces. North Americans generally have a right to build their own cars if they want, and if there is any testing it centres on safety and functionality. Emissions can be a problem in some states, but generally anything that is registered and street legal will remain registered and street legal.

Engine and chassis numbers

The chassis number should match the registration document, and the engine number should also tally with it. We couldn't care less if it's the 'correct' engine number for a replica car, but we do care if the engine turns out to be stolen, and we do care if it turns out to be a much newer engine that therefore requires the fitting of catalytic convertors, fuel-injection and an ECU. In the UK, pre-1972 engines have no emission rules other than not emitting visible smoke, so you can run them with open pipes, evil camshaft profiles, and a forest of Webers for decidedly nippy performance and dreadful emissions. Some newly cast imported V8s with fake old numbers recently attracted the wrong sort of attention in the UK, so be careful with this. An engine number can usually be checked with the manufacturer to establish its age. In most of the world, older engines have emissions exemptions, but checking would be wise.

... it seems to be an early Dax body with a custom chassis. Its Q registration says it's already been correctly registered as a vehicle of unknown year and donors. The UK's Q reg scheme knocks off some value in many people's eyes.

Unleaded fuel

Some engines built before about 1976 don't have hardened exhaust valve seats. If the seats are cut directly into the cast iron of the heads, which was the usual practice for ordinary cars using leaded petrol, they will slowly erode. BMC engines are probably the worst, but American engines can sometimes last for ages. The area that is eroded ends up being cut out anyway when hard seats are eventually fitted, so there's no need to bother about it until you lose power, which happens when you finally run out of compression. It's more money off the offer price, though, unless there's proof that the valve seats have been upgraded.

Oil and coolant

The dipstick tells a story. If the oil is low, thin, runny and black, the car has been neglected. You need to see the correct level of fairly clean oil on the dipstick.

Take the oil filler cap off – if there's a lot of whitish emulsion inside it, there's water in the oil, which suggests that a head gasket has gone, or that the block or a cylinder head is warped. A little emulsion is okay, as it tends to suggest internal condensation and a rarely-used engine. The coolant cap tells the same story – if there's a lot of white cack in the cap and the radiator, there's water in the oil. At best it's a head-off job to replace a failed gasket, at worst it's a new engine.

(Remember to check the radiator cap while the engine is cold. If you take it off while the engine's hot, the steam will instantly scald you.)

Compression test

Even cylinder compressions are a good guide to a sound engine. A tester costs about ●x20 and is screwed into each sparkplug hole in turn. Low compression on one cylinder could be a serious piston problem, or a less serious head problem. Budget for a rebuild, or walk away.

Cold start and hot idle

If the engine is worn, starting it from stone cold is a good way to hear any clattering or tapping from excessive bearing clearances or other wear. If the engine is injected or running on carbs with an electric choke, you need to know that the system is working properly. You also need to leave the car idling until it reaches normal operating temperature and more, and then you want to hear the fan or fans coming in and watch the temperature stabilizing. My own 5.7-litre Cobretti used to brew up like a volcano and spit its hoses off until I got big enough fans on it. Keep the bonnet closed during this test, as an open bonnet is a good aid to cooling: before sorting out the fans, I used to open the back of the bonnet a couple of inches as soon as I saw traffic.

The interior is nicely executed in cream leather, and shows very little wear. The gear lever is manual and has an overdrive switch – these are all good features to have.

Marque-specific design faults

The Cobra replica industry does not frantically produce new and increasingly complex models every year like Toyota, and it doesn't generally overestimate its engineering skills and make design mistakes. Neither does it obsess with scrimping on materials. So, the incidence of mistakes, design faults and mass recalls is much rarer than it is in the world of production cars.

The Cobretti Viper, for example, traces its ancestry thirty years back to the early 1980s and the Sheldonhurst Cobra – its fat front wheelarches are that way because the car was originally designed for German TÜV approval, and had to use its Ford Granada front axle in completely standard full-width form. The Sheldonhurst became the Brightwheel, which was Jag and Chevy-based, then after Brightwheel went bust, the car became the Cobretti. Thirty years later, it's still basically the same car, still very strong and still belt-and-braces over-engineered.

The good news is that with free access to the Cobra Club forum, and to advice from people who build, buy, drive and enjoy the cars on a hands-on basis, you can chat to owners and manufacturers and see if there are any marque-specific problems you should look for – even if it's just that the doors are difficult to line up. If you're thinking about building a car, some are easier than others to construct. Bear in mind that internet information is exactly as reliable as any other gossip, so make sure you listen to (lots of) real owners rather than on-line fantasists who have never even sat in a Cobra.

There's also the matter of your own body shape and size. Unlike standard-issue production car interiors geared to average-sized shoppers, no two Cobra interiors are the same shape, and some will fit you better than others. More good news is that unlike production cars, you can often take a Cobra kit back to its manufacturer and ask them to alter it to fit you. Cobras are bespoke tailoring, rather than factory-outlet, one-size-fits-all product from Hyundai or BMW.

Big old-school Jaguar speedo and tacho are good news, and the rest of the dash is nice, too. Push-button start is cool.

Bodywork

GRP doesn't rust, and any problems that arise with it are relatively easy to deal with, if a little icky. You can see for yourself how smooth the body mouldings are just by crouching down and looking along them. If ten years of rising heat from two big red-hot exhaust manifolds, or minor malformations from ageing moulds have resulted in ripples along the front wings, you can see them. Knock some money off. If you see stress cracks on the inside or the outside of the shell, knock lots of money off, and repair them at your leisure: they don't affect the function of the car, as the body is mostly decorative. When it suits, you can grind them out, add some more gel to the outer surface, more resin and matting to beef up the area from underneath, and repaint.

Panel fit in Cobra replicas can be quite poor, as GRP is plastic which literally means malleable or bendy. (A new bodyshell awaiting fitting must be properly supported, or as it continues to cure, it will sag into a shape that won't fit the chassis when the time comes to put it on.) Each opening panel is made of an inner and outer part, the body is made in a mould constructed from several sections bolted together, and all of it is hand-made – so how well the parts fit together varies by individual car as well as by marque. You can't look at both sides of the car at once anyway, so absolute symmetry is moot. Look at a few cars and decide what you can live with, and how much you want to pay. (In my first Cobretti, the original boot lid didn't fit the repaired body, so I had to cut the inner and outer apart, force the outer boot lid shell into the right shape, and then bond the inner back in to fix it into the new shape. My skills are almost entirely in words and ideas, and I'm short on patience – but even so, I had no problem doing this, and therefore neither would you.)

Crash damage is not a major worry in a car with a solid steel chassis and a decorative GRP body, and in fact I would recommend buying a crashed and salvaged Cobra replica as a bargain if you can find one. My own Cobretti Viper was built from a new chassis and a massively damaged body that was about to be thrown away. I'd been told that repairing GRP was easy, so I decided to have a go, and it genuinely is easy. A quarter of the body was replaced with a new corner, and a shredded front wing was repaired by letting in a new section. Other damage was repaired with matting and resin on the inside and gelcoat on the outside, and the body finished up pretty much as good as new.

Sloppy finishing of obscured inside surfaces is both a reason for knocking money off, and a warning about the general build quality. Look inside the wheelarches, behind the dash, and inside the boot. You don't want to see bubbles, stray strands of glass, thin bits of matting and bad finishing of the tricky areas inside sharp corners where it's difficult to get enough fibres stuffed in with a brush. If there are air bubbles in corners, they may show though the paint in the longer term.

Oh dear. Off comes ●x3000-4000 in value. Rather than a V8, this is the donor Jaguar straight-six. If it's an early 4.2 it's a potential liability, and it sounds wrong in a Cobra. The triple SUs and manifold could be sold to a Jag fan when your V8 goes in.

Chassis ④ ③ ② ①

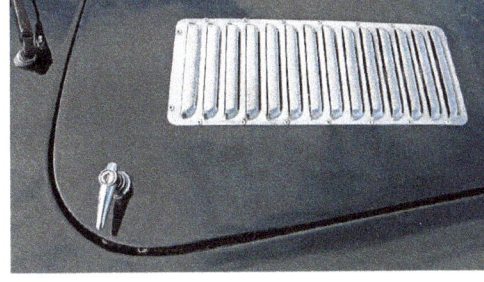

In general, kitcar chassis are too thick to rust through in any timescale that we need to worry about. They are also quite hard to damage: an older Viper once destroyed a Land Rover in an almost head-on crash. The Cobra had significant frontal body damage, a squashed wheel, bent Jaguar wishbones, a cracked screen, and some paint missing from the back of the door. The chassis was stripped, and dropped into the manufacturing jig to see where it was bent ... and it wasn't. The upper

This doesn't work either: riveting louvred plates on without painting them is a bit sloppy. Was the car overheating? Bonnets are also expected to have a scoop.

wishbone mounting bar was bent back an inch or two, that was all. The Cobretti Viper is probably the heaviest and strongest of the Cobra chassis, but the rest of them are pretty tough, too – it's not the same world as crumple-zoned production cars.

The downside of driving an extremely strong structure is that although hitting something soft like a Land Rover is no problem, hitting something hard like a tree is going to hurt. Some crumple-zone effect is provided by the bodywork and radiator/bumper frame, but not much, and there are no airbags.

It also has to be said that kitcar chassis are hand-made in jigs, so the accuracy of their geometry can be as variable as some older production cars. If you measure a chassis cross-corner and it's out of shape, first drive the car and see if the suspension fitment and adjustment has compensated, and the car drives straight and true. Secondly, go and measure a Mini shell. Having digested the resultant shock, decide how much pinpoint accuracy really matters to you.

Wheels and tyres ④ ③ ② ①

The condition of wheels and tyres can tell you a lot. First, check the insides as well as the outsides of both rims and tyres for damage or bulges. Check the age of the tyres: there's a code number on the sidewalls. Google 'tyre age code' to find the info for your country. Tyres should not be used for more than six or seven years, particularly in high-performance cars, although if they're kept on a lightweight car in a dark garage, and used regularly enough to avoid flat-spotting damage, they could last longer. (The actual problem is that they eventually go hard and lose grip.) Replacing old tyres could cost between ●x1000 and ●x2000.

Wear patterns on tyres can tell you quite a lot. If tyres are worn in the middle or on both outside edges, that means poor maintenance, incorrect tyre pressures, and a careless or ill-informed owner. Over-inflation makes the tyre bulge into a bagel shape so it only runs on the middle of the tread, and under-inflation means it's squashy and flat so the outer edges wear more quickly.

If the inside or outside edges of the front tyre tread are worn much more than the middle and opposite side, the wheels are not running parallel, and are probably either pointing too far inwards or outwards. This is usually remedied by a simple adjustment of the front tracking, and not a worry if a tracking check confirms that the wheels were out of adjustment. If the tyres are worn on one side and the tracking checks out to be correct, there could be a camber issue.

Camber is how far out the bottom of the wheel is from the car, compared to the top of the wheel. A little negative camber (wheels sloping inwards at the top) is good, because the tyre deforms slightly into a desirable shape on cornering. When the car is stuffed into a left-hand corner with enthusiasm and a little negative camber, centrifugal forces compete with grip to make the right front tyre tread sit flat on the road. Lots of negative camber gets you better cornering, but the downside is that on the straight, the tyres are not vertical so the insides wear faster than the outside edges. On Minis, one degree of negative camber is a good compromise between tyre wear and grip, so that may help as a guide.

If just one tyre (of a matched pair on either axle) is worn on the outside or inside, that suggests the suspension on that corner is bent or otherwise out of true. That wheel is at the wrong angle compared to the rest. If the rear tyres are worn unevenly, the suspension is either tired, damaged, or out of true.

These problems can simply be due to maladjustment, but a full alignment check would be wise before buying the car. If you're serious about buying a car and you suspect it has suspension alignment issues, a full check is definitely worth doing. Usually there will be enough adjustment in kitcar suspension to get both ends straightened out, but if not, you're looking at some relatively major work. It can be done, but check the potential cost before making your offer.

The wheels are ancient Wolfrace alloys with an unaggressive offset to suit the wide Jag axles. I'd start off with an offer under ●x10,000. It's odd and old, but it's a nice car.

Brakes

A complete donor braking system is a cheap and very effective solution. It's already balanced with nearly all the braking taking place at the front, and any production-car brake system in a kit car that's half the weight of the donor car has twice as much braking as it needs. You may not want to use the standard servo, if the donor brake system comes with one. I once had to remove a kitcar brake servo because the front wheels locked as soon as the pedal was touched.

So, pretty much all Cobra replicas have brakes that are twice as powerful as they need to be, but fancier Cobra replicas are likely to have branded brakes that are more than twice as powerful. There's an element of fashion here: a Timex watch tells the time just fine, but most people would rather have a fairly expensive fake Breitling or a ludicrously expensive real one. (Funnily enough, at a gathering of friends whose car collection is worth a collective several million dollars, all were wearing fake expensive watches except me – I was wearing a plain but genuine Raymond Weil. On the other hand, their cars are real and mine have mostly been fakes.)

If you're going to hammer regularly on a small-block V8 Cobra during track days and find you really do need more brakes, Wilwood seems to offer good value as an upgrade. They're not fashionable enough for tuner kids, but they do a good job of stopping fast cars for a reasonable price. If you use replica Halibrand wheels you can even retain drums at the back – they work more than well enough, and you can't see them through the wheels anyway if they're painted matt black.

Check the brake discs for wear and condition. You can't check for warping by looking, but pulsing at the pedal in time with wheel rotation can mean warped discs. Not a big deal, but more money off the price, please. Ask the owner to demonstrate the brakes somewhere safe, and see if you're happy with the stopping power, and that the car stops in a straight line.

Suspension

There used to be a Lister spring conversion kit available for the Jaguar XJS that managed to make it both harsh and soggy at the same time. Spring and shock rates offer many options for mistakes, but are easy to adapt to suit your driving. Springs are quite cheaply available in any length, size and rating, and most shocks fitted to Cobra replicas are adjustable. One possible problem is that shocks may not go soft enough for a light car, but advice from Cobra manufacturers is freely available. Something worth knowing is that Lotus's Colin Chapman always used soft springing and hard shocks as the best combination for going quickly and smoothly. If you don't like the suspension on a particular Cobra replica, but love the rest of the car, it's not a big problem to sort out.

These are the most desirable wheels you can find on a Cobra replica. Halibrand replicas, pin drive, with wired spinners. The spinners are too 'dangerous' to pass SVA, but legal securing methods can be used.

Drivability

This isn't much of an issue with production cars, as pedal weights, gear lever action, switch positioning and so on are part of a five-year design process, and have to remain within a small range to be acceptable for Mr and Mrs Average. However, these parameters can be quite random in unique cars constructed with parts from different sources, and can also be random between different examples of the same marque. You have to be happy with the whole feel of the car, or budget for changing it.

When evaluating the performance and handling of the car, first go for a ride as a passenger – the owner will normally be happy to show you something of what the car is capable of, once you've established that he's not a fool who's going to kill you. When you drive the car yourself, you're not looking for its limits – you're judging whether you will still enjoy it when the novelty has worn off.

For example, the 1991 Southern Roadcraft V8 demonstrator had a brutally heavy clutch, which was apparently designed to be too heavy for wives to operate. It was a lovely car to drive, but after half an hour I was more or less only using third gear as my leg was aching. Dax's V12 Jaguar-engined Tojeiro demo had a small steering wheel, and steering so heavy I don't want to drive another one.

All older American four-speed manual gearboxes are hard work: they're capable of handing 500lb-ft of torque from a big-block, because the components are all heavy-duty commercial truck parts. Forget about snatched changes; you're waiting for huge gears to trundle along immense shafts and thud into place like lock gates.

You might thoroughly enjoy the massive feel of a big-block and its agricultural gearbox, of course, but you'll have to try one over some distance to find out.

Steering too heavy? Use smaller tyres, and change the steering wheel for a big Moto-Lita. Monster sticky tyres add considerably to steering weight, and can also foul up handling and road feel as they skitter over bumps and try to follow white lines. The wide-arched Cobretti Viper and its ancestors use full-width Jaguar axles and relatively narrow tyres, so they're very sure-footed, the crucially important contact patch between tyre and road is well weighted, and their steering is nicely light. Looking favourably upon the all-alloy Rover V8 is also a smart move when building or buying nice drivable cars, as the Rover weighs no more than an iron four-cylinder engine.

Clutch too heavy? You can change the relationship of the bores of the master and slave cylinders, and you can move the pivot point of the pedal for more leverage. You can even add a servo, although it starts getting complicated at this point. Up to 250bhp you shouldn't need a serious performance clutch, so if the pedal is heavy there's a flaw in the design somewhere.

Does the car have sidepipes? These make a big statement, but you can only hear half the engine and you'll be deaf in one ear after a run, so you may find yourself longing for an under-floor system before long.

Does the car have weather gear? Are sidescreens included with the soft top? Hard plastic or glass sliding sidescreens are a major bonus, because without them you get quite a battering from the slipstream coming round the side of the windscreen. There are now three different sorts of detachable tops available – the original Spitfire-style bubble top, and two Le Mans-style long tops that make Cobra replicas much more waterproof and genuinely capable of grand touring rather than just grandstanding.

Before road-testing a powerful car, make sure that either your own insurance covers you for driving other cars, or that the seller's insurance covers any driver and is current.

Electrics   4 3 2 1

This is nice and simple. Either things work or they don't. If you see Scotchloks in the wiring, that's not a good sign. Also look for tidiness and a neatly wrapped wiring loom, and check behind the dashboard for either clipped neatness or multi-coloured spaghetti. Take a tape or CD to check out the sound system. You won't be able to hear it over the engine anyway, but it's another thing over which to chew your lips and look doubtful.

A Backdraft – a well-known manufacturer, and the car is in the favourite colours with a very good specification level. This will command a good price.

Build quality   4 3 2 1

Cobra replicas, and Cobras before them, have always been hand-made cars. That excuses some degree of unreliability compared to Japanese shopping cars, but things can still be well-built by hand or badly-built by hand. Most of these hand-made kits are also amateur-assembled, so you're going to get the same variability of workmanship as any DIY work: if you look at how the car is assembled and can see the equivalent of a shelf duct-taped to a wall, you can either walk away or you can regard the car in front of you as a temporarily assembled object which will need to be taken apart again and then put together properly. Make an offer based on that judgement, or walk away.

The builder may have done things like re-using Nylocks: if you don't know what that means, you need to educate yourself about fasteners before you consider buying a home-built car or building one yourself. This is not a mistake restricted to amateurs: it was a 'professional' mechanic who once cheaped out on a new Nylock, resulting in the wheel of a Cobra replica falling off as a suspension wishbone came adrift.

Look behind the dashboard. Is the dash panel itself held on by little bolts, nuts and washers, or by cheap self-tapping screws?

Look under the car at the piping, which is a good clue as to general build quality. The fuel and brake lines are secured by clips. Are they equally spaced? Are there plenty of them, and are they the right size? Has the piping itself been carefully bent around jam pots, jack handles, and so on in a pleasing set of neat bends, or is it all a bit haphazard where it's not on view?

Fuel system

Check for leaks, for well-made and fairly large-bore fuel piping, and silicone sealer used around the fuel cap. (This dissolves and then reappears later in the carbs as 'gorilla snot.') Check that the fuel tank is in a safe place, ideally above the axle, and that there is nothing at the back of the car that could punch a hole in the tank if you're rear-ended. If the engine is old enough it probably doesn't need a catalytic convertor or electronic fuel injection, which is good news, as it can run a variety of carbs. Carter and Holley carbs are cheap, simple and effective, while four Italian twin-chokes with polished trumpets are much more glamorous – but if they don't already run well, tuning them is like herding cats. Check that electric choke systems function properly from a cold start. They work by bending bi-metallic strips, so they will fail sooner or later. I prefer a manual choke that can be turned off as soon as the engine can run without it. Manual conversion is usually easy.

The Backdraft's interior follows through with the same quality as the outside – black leather, nice wheel, instruments, and harnesses.

Methods of payment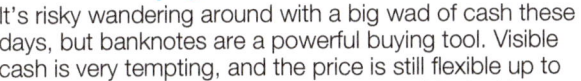

It's risky wandering around with a big wad of cash these days, but banknotes are a powerful buying tool. Visible cash is very tempting, and the price is still flexible up to the moment when you hand over some of it. Just be aware of where you are.

Bank drafts are a safe way to pay, but there are fakes around, so I wouldn't let a car go unless I had seen the draft being issued at the bank. Other people may begin to think this way. If you buy from a dealer, using a credit card is wise as it offers some useful protection.

Offering to pay for the fuel used in a long test is a good idea: it says you're serious about buying the car, and it makes a long test run a reasonable request.

Take it for an inspection

Most countries have some sort of a tech inspection system, and it's mostly state-run and good value compared to a private inspection. For Brits, the MoT test is excellent value for anybody buying any car. ●x55 gets you a good mechanical going-over, up on a ramp where you can usually, unofficially, join the examiner under the car and get a good look at everything. It's a rare treat for an MoT tester to get to look at something exotic rather than his daily diet of baggy Toyotas, so a Cobra replica will get his full attention.

The UK's MoT test covers the body and vehicle structure, steering, suspension, brakes, emissions, windscreen, wipers/washers, lighting, door/bonnet/boot operation, seatbelts, seat mountings, mirrors, horn, exhaust system condition and noise level, fuel system, tyres, wheels and registration plates.

While MoT testers' expertise is variable, any serious mistakes in assembly are likely to be spotted, together with worn or damaged suspension components, uneven brakes, fluid leaks, damage to tyres and wheels on the insides, insecure brake or fuel lines, and many other things that you might have missed during your own inspection.

If the car passes the test, that's good news, and the price should be unaffected – surely the seller expected it to be roadworthy in the first place?

If it fails, the seller is at a psychological disadvantage, and has no good reason for not adjusting the price downwards to reflect the cost of the repairs. Sidepipes are a likely fail on the basis of noise: quieter sidepipes can be bought, and I have in the past quietened an exhaust by stuffing the tailpipes with wire wool.

An extra bonus of going through a government test as part of a car examination is that the garage's computer may well flag up anything dodgy in the car's registration.

Carpets and trim

This is either in good condition or not. If the trim is leather, something to consider for the longer term is that black and dark-coloured leather looks more inviting with age and patina, whereas magnolia leather doesn't. Cheap Cobra seats can get quite uncomfortable quite quickly, and may not have any lumbar support at all, so try to sit in them long enough to check whether you get backache.

Evaluation procedure
Add up the total points score:

84 = excellent, possibly concours; 63 = good; 42 = average; 21 = poor.

Cars scoring over 59 will be completely useable and will require only maintenance and care to keep in condition. Cars scoring between 21 and 43 will require full restoration (at much the same cost again as buying the car), cars scoring between 44 and 58 will require very careful assessment of necessary repair/restoration costs in order to reach a realistic value.

10 Auctions
– sold! Another way to buy your dream

It's quite rare for a Cobra replica to come up at auction, but you could save thousands so it's worth keeping your eyes on the auction listings via the internet.

This is a fairly recent AK, a car with a good reputation. Colour, sidepipes, Halibrand replica wheels, V8 are all correct, and condition is excellent. My mental limit for an auction bid would be ●x15,000, and somebody else would probably pay much more.

Auction pros & cons
Pros: Prices will usually be lower than those of dealers or private sellers and you might grab a real bargain on the day. Auctioneers have usually established clear title with the seller. At the venue you can usually examine documentation relating to the vehicle.
Cons: You have to rely on a sketchy catalogue description of condition and history. The opportunity to inspect is limited and you cannot drive the car. Auction cars are often a little below par and may require some work. It's easy to overbid. There will usually be a buyer's premium to pay in addition to the auction hammer price.

Which auction?
Established auctioneers advertise in car magazines and on the auction houses' websites. A catalogue, or a simple printed list of the lots for auctions might only be available a day or two ahead, though often lots are listed and pictured on auctioneers' websites much earlier. Contact the auction company to ask if previous auction selling prices are available as this is useful information (details of past sales are often available on websites).

Catalogue, entry fee and payment details

When you buy the catalogue of the vehicles in the auction, it often acts as a ticket allowing two people to attend the viewing days and the auction. Catalogue details tend to be comparatively brief, but will include information such as 'one owner from new, low mileage, full service history,' etc. It will also usually show a guide price to give you some idea of what to expect to pay and will tell you what is charged as a 'buyer's premium.' The catalogue will also contain details of acceptable forms of payment. At the fall of the hammer an immediate deposit is usually required, the balance payable within 24 hours. If the plan is to pay by cash there may be a cash limit. Some auctions will accept payment by debit card. Sometimes credit or charge cards are acceptable, but will often incur an extra charge. A bank draft or bank transfer will have to be arranged in advance with your own bank as well as with the auction house. No car will be released before all payments are cleared. If delays occur in payment transfers, storage costs can accrue.

Buyer's premium

A buyer's premium will be added to the hammer price: don't forget this in your calculations. It is not usual for there to be further tax on the purchase price and/or on the buyer's premium in the UK.

Viewing

In some instances it's possible to view on the day, or days before, as well as in the hours prior to, the auction. There are auction officials available who will help out by opening engine and luggage compartments and to allow you to inspect the interior. While the officials may start the engine for you, a test drive is out of the question. Crawling under and around the car as much as you want is permitted, but you can't suggest that the car you are interested in be jacked up, or attempt to do the job yourself. You can also ask to see any documentation available.

Bidding

Before you take part in the auction, decide your maximum bid – and stick to it!
 It may take a while for the auctioneer to reach the lot you are interested in, so use that time to observe how other bidders behave. When it's the turn of your car, attract the auctioneer's attention and make an early bid. The auctioneer will then look to you for a reaction every time another bid is made. Usually the bids will be in fixed increments until the bidding slows, when smaller increments will often be accepted before the hammer falls. If you want to withdraw from the bidding, make sure the auctioneer understands your intentions – a vigorous shake of the head when he or she looks to you for the next bid should do the trick! Assuming that you are the successful bidder, the auctioneer will note your card or paddle number, and from that moment on you will be responsible for the vehicle.If the car is unsold, either because it failed to reach the reserve or because there was little interest, it may be possible to negotiate with the owner, via the auctioneers, after the sale is over.

Successful bid

There are two more items to think about. How to get the car home, and insurance. If you can't drive the car, your own or a hired trailer is one option, and another is to have the vehicle shipped using the facilities of a local company. The auction house will have details of companies specialising in the transfer of cars.

I built this Cobretti to suit myself, and my choices damage its value. The turbo 400 auto tranny and the Chevy Camaro wheels both knock off value – but at auction, nobody would know I had built it with a smashed and reclaimed body. Caveat emptor.

Insurance for immediate cover can usually be purchased on site, but it may be more cost-effective to make arrangements with your own insurance company in advance, and then call to confirm the full details.

eBay & other online auctions

eBay & other online auctions could land you a car at a bargain price, though you'd be foolhardy to bid without examining the car first, something most vendors encourage. A useful feature of eBay is the geographical location of the car is shown, so you can narrow your choices to those within a realistic radius of home. Be prepared to be outbid in the last few moments of the auction. Remember, your bid is binding and that it will be very, very difficult to get restitution in the case of a crooked vendor fleecing you – caveat emptor!

Be aware that some cars offered for sale in online auctions are 'ghost' cars. Don't part with any cash without being sure that the vehicle does actually exist and is as described (usually pre-bidding inspection is possible).

Auctioneers

Barrett-Jackson
www.barrett-jackson.com
Bonhams www.bonhams.com
British Car Auctions (BCA)
www.bca-europe.com or
www.british-car-auctions.co.uk
Cheffins www.cheffins.co.uk

Christies www.christies.com
Coys www.coys.co.uk
eBay www.ebay.com
H&H www.classic-auctions.co.uk
RM www.rmauctions.com
Shannons www.shannons.com.au
Silver www.silverauctions.com

11 Paperwork
– correct documentation is essential!

Classic, collector and prestige cars usually come with a large portfolio of paperwork accumulated and passed on by a succession of proud owners. This documentation represents some of the history of the car, and from it can be deduced the level of care the car has received, and how much it's been used. All this information will be potentially useful to you as the new owner, so be very wary of cars with little paperwork to support their claimed history. Kit replicas correctly registered in the last few years require a photographic record of their build, so you will want these photos, or copies of them, to be supplied with the car.

This Cobretti Viper has just passed the SVA test. Note the 'safe' hub caps, the 'safe' Jaguar steering wheel, the fog light and indicator side repeaters, and the naff mirrors with 'safe' radiused edges.

Correct registration

Cobra replicas can present complications if incorrectly registered – not insurmountable, but potentially expensive.

My first kit car was a Midge, built in about 1985. It used a Triumph Vitesse for a donor, and had a new chassis. It was inspected at my home by an official who said it was very nice, and gave me a new chassis number. The car is now a tax-free 1971 Triumph Midge and needs an annual MoT. Easy.

Many people built a Jag-based Cobra with a new body and chassis, sent the registration book in to have it altered to read 'Jaguar Sports' or some such, got an MoT and carried on driving it with the same VIN number. There was an amnesty for these cars, but it has expired. Any car of this type will get caught at an MoT test, and will probably now need to pass a current IVA test, which it was never designed for. It's possible, but at a price. Headlamp height and seatbelt anchorage height can present interesting challenges.

Currently, the UK test costs around ●x500, and while some aspects of it are reassuring and sensible, much of it is Elf'n'Safety idiocy: a spare wheel mounted externally has to be covered up with a piece of board as well as a cover, in case the dangerously sharp rim edge cuts a pedestrian if you reverse into them – but the other identical rims on the outside of the car are apparently safe. Best to avoid the test if possible.

These grotesque seat extensions are a good idea, I have to reluctantly admit, and would help with back and neck injuries when rear-ended. They're not legally required yet.

UK kitcar registration currently follows several routes.

Category A is **amateur-built** cars. Amateur status must be proved by pictures of you assembling the car. Emissions are based on provable engine age. A donor car kit will get an age related number plate, and a new component kit (with one major older component allowed, usually the engine) gets a current registration number. Receipts for everything must be produced.

Category C is **professionally built**. The engine and one other major component can be old. Engine-age emissions exemptions apply.

Category L is a **complete new car** built by a low-volume manufacturer. It will be tested to current emissions standards.

So, if the registration is older but correct, with the kit brand name mentioned and a replacement chassis number issued, no worries. If the car is correctly registered within one of the new categories, no worries. If neither applies, knock ●x1000-2000 off for getting it through IVA, or walk away.

Registration documents

All countries/states have some form of registration for private vehicles, whether it's like the American 'pink slip' system or the British 'registration document' system.

It is essential to check that the registration document is genuine, that it relates to the car in question, and that all the vehicle's details are correctly recorded, including chassis/VIN and engine numbers (if these are shown). If you are buying from the previous owner, their name and address will be recorded in the document: this will not be the case if you are buying from a dealer. In the UK the current (Euro-aligned) registration document is named "V5C", and is printed in coloured sections of blue, green and pink. The blue section relates to the car specification, the green section has details of the new owner and the pink section is sent to the DVLA in the UK when the car is sold. A small section in yellow deals with selling the car within the motor trade.In the UK the DVLA will provide details of earlier keepers of the vehicle upon payment of a small fee, and much can be learned in this way. French authorities dislike kit cars, and have elevated obstructive bureaucracy to an art form. In Canada, manufacturing kit cars is illegal, but making U-built cars is fine. The USA has a long tradition of registering hot rods, and organisations exist to fight off bureaucracy.

If you're building a kit Cobra, keep photos of everything you do, and hang on to the donor car's VIN plate. Your Cobra will get a new VIN number when it's built.

Roadworthiness certificate

Most country/state administrations require that vehicles are regularly tested to prove that they are safe to use on the public highway and do not produce excessive emissions. In the UK that test (the 'MoT') is carried out at approved testing stations, for a fee. In the USA the requirement varies, but most states insist on an emissions test every two years as a minimum, while the police are charged with pulling over unsafe-looking vehicles.

In the UK the test is required on an annual basis once a vehicle becomes three years old. MoT certificates include the mileage reading recorded each year, and become part of the car's history. Ask the seller if previous certificates are available. Without an MoT the vehicle should be trailered to its new home, unless you insist on MoT testing the car as part of the deal. This is an excellent idea, as it's a good and cheap general inspection and a failure reduces the car's value. If the owner refuses to allow the car to be tested, that's suspicious.

Road licence

The administration of every country/state charges some kind of tax for the use of its road system. The actual form of the 'road licence' and how it is displayed varies widely from country to country and state to state.

Whatever the form of the 'road licence,' it must relate to the vehicle carrying it, and must be present and valid if the car is to be driven on the public highway legally. The value of the licence will depend on the length of time it remains valid. In the UK if a car is untaxed because it has not been used for a period of time, the owner has to inform the licencing authorities. Changed legislation in the UK means that the seller of a car must surrender any existing road fund licence, and it is the responsibility of the new owner to re-tax the vehicle at the time of purchase and before the car can be driven on the road. It's therefore vital to see the Vehicle Registration Certificate (V5C) at the time of purchase, and to have access to the New Keeper Supplement (V5C/2), allowing the buyer to obtain road tax immediately. Some earlier Cobra replicas with period registrations qualify for this valuable concession. In the UK a car not on the road must be recorded as being off the road with a SORN certificate. If you buy a car it must be taxed or SORNed immediately. UK government fines start from ●x80 and rise to ●x1000, plus potential clamping and having your vehicle crushed or sold if you do not comply.

Service history

Often these cars will have been serviced at home by enthusiastic (and hopefully capable) owners. Nevertheless, try to obtain as many receipts and other paperwork pertaining to the car as you can. Items such as the original bill of sale, build manual, parts invoices and repair bills add to the story and the character of the car. A sales brochure is a useful document and something that you could well have to search hard to locate in future years.

If the seller claims to have carried out regular servicing, ask what work was completed, when, and seek some evidence of it being carried out. Your assessment of the car's overall condition should tell you whether the seller's claims are genuine.

Here's a good way of achieving more than the required seatbelt mounting height. If you were to hit anything hard enough for the seatbelt to bend the rollover bar, your head would be elsewhere anyway.

12 What's it worth?
– let your head rule your heart

This orange paint job would probably make the car very difficult to sell. If you're buying, do the sums and make an offer minus the cost of a repaint in conventional colours.

How close a replica is it?
The most saleable and valuable Cobra replica looks and sounds exactly like the real thing. The least valuable is a wildly individual low-budget car in which the builder has indulged his own peculiar tastes. That is the best part of building your own car, of course, but the individualist builder has to understand that there is a price to pay when it comes to market value.

Desirable options/extras
High-status manufacturer. Standard Cobra colours – metallic blue with white stripes. An American V8. (Big-blocks are the most macho and carry a premium for some people. Ford 289s and 302s come next, followed by the Chevrolet 350 – it's a cheaper, stronger and better engine, but the AC Cobra always used

The most ubiquitous UK Cobra replica engine is the aluminium Rover V8, for good reason – it's light, cheap, available, and powerful enough.

A newly finished Dax is at the top of the tree for UK values. If it has a new registration it won't need an MoT for a while.

This Hawk 289 is a pretty authentic replica but for the dashboard. Even the tail-lights are correct. However, more than 90 per cent of Cobra buyers want a fat 427-shaped monster, so 289 fans are an elite minority – it could take a while to sell one.

45

Ford engines.) Rover V8 is quite well accepted. Trendy performance brand names on the engine. Alloy cylinder heads on US V8s. A manual gearbox. Jaguar axles. Uprated big-name brakes. Leather trim. Accuracy of replication – Halibrand replica wired knock-off wheels, Moto-Lita steering wheel, replica Smiths clocks on a plank dashboard. Weather gear.

Undesirable features

Low-budget manufacturer. Unattractive and non-metallic colours. Gelcoat rather than paint. Vinyl interior. An engine that's not a V8, such as a V6 or a four-cylinder. (My own new Cobra replica design uses a violently turbocharged four-cylinder, but I'm also quietly leaving room in the engine bay for a V8.) A Jaguar V12: extremely heavy, too smooth and makes the wrong noise, but some like it. An autobox. Mixed interior styling – modern steering wheels with old-school clocks. Recycled donor instruments, unless they're chrome-rimmed 5in Jaguar clocks. Unusual fashionable wheels.

Condition

It's unusual to find a Cobra replica in bad condition – they're hand-built, usually treasured, and rarely driven if it looks like rain. You're looking for bad or amateurish construction rather than corrosion or damage.

Once you've seen a few cars, you'll get a feel for how well they're been assembled and finished. It would be worth educating yourself in nut and bolt markings – if somebody's used a coach bolt where they should have used a setscrew and Nylock, it's a guide to their skill, knowledge and general approach. The construction of brake lines and fittings is also revealing. How does the car you have in mind compare with generally advertised prices for that replica marque? If the price is way high don't bother, and conversely if the price looks too good to be true, it probably is.

This Pilgrim is low-budget, with a pedestrian four-cylinder Ford Pinto engine. I'd be looking to pay around ●x10,000 for a Pinto Pilgrim.

The view from the office of the same budget Pilgrim could be that of a car that cost ●x5000 more – all it needs is a better engine. Even a V6 would be an improvement.

This is another Pilgrim, but this time with what looks like a standard Rover V8. With the right engine fitted, it's worth several thousand more – and it doesn't cost that much to find and fit a good Rover engine.

Fitting a V8 entitles you to use sidepipes, easily retro-fitted. A single sidepipe with a four-cylinder engine is just sad.

Before you start haggling with the seller, consider what effect any variation from ideal specifications might have on the car's future value. If you are buying from a dealer, remember there will be a dealer's premium on the price.

Striking a deal

Negotiate on the basis of your condition assessment, mileage, and the cost of having things re-done your way. Decide how badly the owner needs the money. My second (Ford Cortina-based) Cobra replica was bought very cheaply because it had a very expensive, almost full-race Pinto engine, and a trick automatic gearbox. I told the owner to keep the engine and box, and made an almost insulting offer on the rest of the car, which was accepted. It helped that I didn't really want it much, having been spoilt by my previous Chevy/Jag Cobretti. I added white stripes and a Rover V8, and sold the car fairly quickly.

Be realistic about the value, but don't be completely intractable. A small compromise on the part of the vendor or buyer will often facilitate a deal.

Corvette LS1 would make a top Cobra engine: all aluminium, 5.7 litres, 350bhp. It would add a premium to value, but not for Ford diehards.

Having rubbished four-cylinder Cobra replicas, why fit a Mazda MX5 engine in my own? Because the turbo/propane system will get me over 500bhp/ton, compared to the Ferrari Enzo's 434bhp/ton. And I'm quietly designing the engine bay to take a V8, too.

13 Do you want to build or buy?
– building will take longer and cost more than you think ...

If you have reasonable mechanical skills and patience, but are restricted by a small budget, you can do very well by taking advantage of somebody else's misfortune and buying an abandoned project. There is a dangerous 90 per cent completed stage in any car project, when people simply get fed up with the whole thing. Wives get sick of being abandoned for a year's worth of evenings. Recession, redundancy and children show up. ●x12,000 worth of hoarded parts and a mostly-finished car can be bought for half that.

Potential problems include pre-IVA kits that can be hard to get through the test, manufacturers going out of business, unused hydraulic cylinders rusting in damp garage storage, and the statistical inevitability that some builders are idiots. You may have to take the car apart completely and start again – not necessarily a bad thing.

Cobretti's Jag-based chassis is heavier and stronger than most, but still shows you roughly what is delivered to your driveway when you order a kit.

My own car's body was written-off, then retrieved and repaired by letting in new sections to replace the damaged areas. It was no big deal, and the body ended up just as strong as a new one would have been.

The author in 1991, getting stuck in and dismantling bits of dead XJ6 in John Gordon's Jaguar scrapyard. You can get hands-on and scrap a Jag yourself, or you can order a donor package and stay clean.

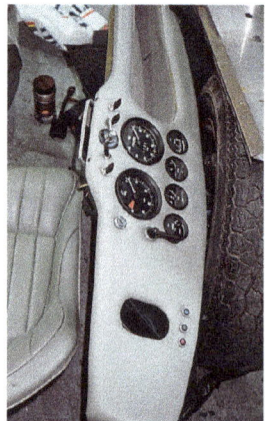

I was lucky enough to find a complete secondhand Cobra interior, and just had to sort out instruments and switchgear.

Moving our sights up a little from abandoned projects, a budget manufacturer such as Pilgrim can sell you a comprehensive Sumo kit with almost everything you need but the donor, for a good price. Pilgrim's Ford V6 package can be used to get a new Cobra replica on the road for ●x12,000 – and that number does add up.

A good point here is that you could run a Sumo in its shiny self-coloured gelcoat with a V6 until you can afford a Rover V8, a nice paint job, and some sidepipes. Pilgrim's construction manual and build video would be an excellent investment at this point. If it all looks too scary, now's the time to back out.

Pilgrim interiors are well developed now, and can be less posh or more posh according to budget. I wouldn't recommend choosing a cream interior on a car you plan to use much, though.

Cooling is always important with a big engine in a small car. Buy good quality fans and avoid Chinese copies. Flex-a-Lite is an American company that takes its quality control seriously.

You have to be able to assemble things, glue things, adjust things, lift things and scramble around and under things in order to build a car, but if you can achieve successful and tidy household DIY you can probably succeed. There is much satisfaction in doing so.

The Chevy 350 in my daily-driver '58 Delray is my favourite engine. Cheap to buy and upgrade, tough, powerful, unchanged for decades, but heavy at 550lb. With ally heads it matches the Ford 302's 460lb – the Rover is much lighter at around 300lb.

The first prototype chassis for the current Ayrspeed – the wide tunnel provides good torsional rigidity, and the engine is well back in the chassis for good balance.

If, on reflection, you don't have the time or patience to learn these skills, there are enough finished Cobras out there to offer you plenty of choice. The smart move is to join a Cobra club and/or your local kit car club, and find some members within reach. Will they want to waste their Saturday helping to find you a car? Damn right they will, it's all part of the fun for them. Definitely take somebody with black fingernails with you when you inspect a car.

Economic depressions aren't all bad: Boeing's lack of orders has bought down the price of carbon fibre and increased its availability, which means I can use it to make my bodies significantly lighter and stiffer, and therefore faster.

GD's body is detachable in an hour, which means it's also attachable in an hour. A GD would be an easy car to build well.

Shell Valley's cutaway show car gives a useful instant view of its approach to Cobra replicas: not high-tech, but good value.

If there's a local small garage or mobile mechanic with a good reputation, that's who you want servicing and repairing your Cobra. There's no computer diagnostic port for main dealers to plug your credit card into – if you have a Pilgrim, it's a Ford in a posh frock, and if it's an AK it's a Jag with a Chevy Camaro engine. The local guy with an apprenticeship and a small workshop is who you're looking for.

If the casino of buying privately is unappealing, there are several kitcar dealers advertising in the UK magazines such as Sovereign and Totalheadturners, and they offer financing and the security of buying from people who need to protect their reputations in the small world of specialist cars.

It will be convenient if you're happy with a very popular FFR or Pilgrim car, because the amount of support and club action for them is excellent, and the assembly process has been streamlined.

14 Paint problems
– bad complexion, including dimples, pimples and bubbles ...

Paint faults on Cobra replicas are generally due to poor paint preparation or inexperience with painting GRP. Their bodywork is made of glass matting and chemically cured plastic resin, which although strong and corrosion-proof, presents its own paint problems. Some of the following conditions may be present in the car you're looking at:

Gelcoat fading
Some Cobras are supplied with a polished, coloured gelcoat instead of paint. This is tough and thick and saves the cost of a paint job, but the colours can fade, particularly red colours since cadmium has been withdrawn. The same problem can apply to painted finishes. Cutting back with mildly abrasive compounds can sometimes bring the finish back to life.

What's wrong with this car? The colours are spot on, but the real Cobra has an aluminium bonnet riveted to a steel frame, with the scoop riveted on as well. As this is a GRP bonnet, the rivets are purely cosmetic, but a nice touch.

Orange peel
This appears as an uneven paint surface, and looks like the tiny dimples on orange skins. It's caused by the failure of atomized paint droplets to blend when they hit the surface. If the paint's thick enough, you can sometimes rub it down to a good finish with rubbing compound or extremely fine grades of wet and dry paper. Knock the cost of a repaint off your offer anyway.

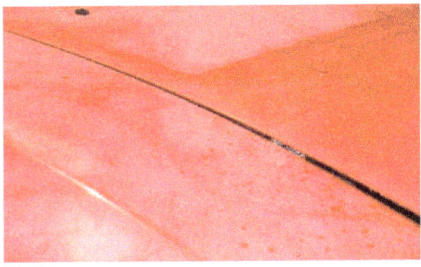

Fading.

Cracking and crazing
This is cracking, fine crazing or a 'crackle' effect like an MGB dashboard. Severe cases are probably caused by too much paint, or too much filler beneath the paint. Inadequate paint-stirring is another possible cause, as is chemical reaction with previous layers of paint. Back down to the gelcoat and start again, I'm afraid.

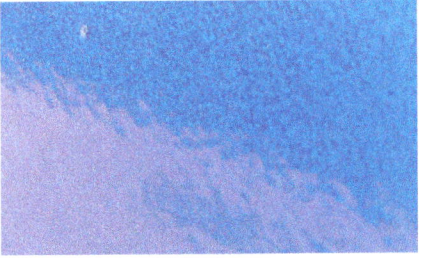

Orange peel.

Star crazing

A stone thrown up in a wheelarch can create a star-shaped crack that spreads out from the point of impact. The repair involves grinding out the cracks and making a gelcoat repair. Before using a GRP car on the road, protect the inner wing surfaces with clear flexible underseal. (Don't use black underseal, as it can leach through and stain the gelcoat.)

Micro blistering exposes the primer beneath.

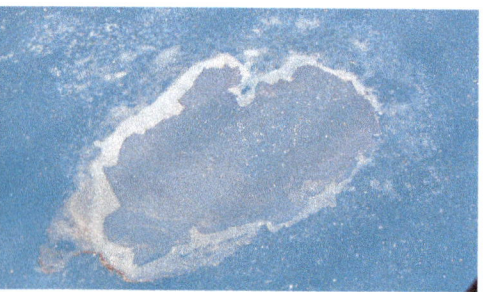

Peeling paint/laquer.

No chance of paint problems with this wild West Coast car, as the paint job probably cost more than some people's entire Cobra budgets.

Blistering

Usually caused by chemical reactions beneath the paint. Has to be taken back to gelcoat, and an isolating primer should be applied before the respray.

Micro-blistering

Usually the result of an amateur or back-yard respray where inadequate heating has allowed moisture to settle on the car before spraying. Consult a paint specialist, but usually damaged paint will have to be removed before partial or full respraying. Micro-blistering can also be caused by car covers that don't 'breathe.' Cheap tarpaulins can also leach chemicals into paint. (As I know to my cost.)

Peeling

Often a problem with metallic and two-pack paintwork when the sealing clearcoat laquer becomes damaged and begins to peel off. Poorly applied paint may also peel. The remedy is to strip and start again.

Dimples or Fisheyes

Dimples in the paintwork on GRP cars are frequently caused by residues of polish (particularly silicone types) or mould wax not being removed properly before painting. Paint removal and repainting is the only solution.

Steel car bodywork is inert unless it's rusting, but GRP is a chemical plastic material: it's wise to use an isolating primer rather than ordinary primer when painting GRP cars, to avoid any chemical reactions.

15 Problems due to lack of use
– just like their owners, Cobra replicas need exercise!

Cars, like humans, work better if exercised regularly. Driving at least ten miles, once a week, is recommended. It's also good for your soul.

Brake systems need to be used and regularly flushed with fresh brake fluid to keep them in good condition. This little-used but rusty wheel cylinder is scrap.

Seized components
Pistons in brake callipers, master and slave cylinders can seize. Clutches may seize if the plate sticks to the flywheel because of corrosion, although once freed it's usually fine. The gearbox may need removal to rectify this. Handbrakes (parking brakes) can seize if the cables and linkages rust or if the rear brake linings stick to the drums. Pistons can seize in engine cylinder bores due to corrosion.

Fluids
Old, acidic oil can corrode bearings, and also deposits icky cack (a technical term) in the sump. Old or uninhibited coolant can corrode internal waterways, particularly in aluminium engines. Lack of antifreeze in coolant can cause core (freeze) plugs to be pushed out, and can even crack blocks or heads. Silt settling and solidifying in radiator tubes and blocking water passages can cause overheating. Brake fluid absorbs water from the atmosphere and should be renewed every two years. Old fluid with a high water content causes the pistons in callipers and wheel cylinders to seize, and can cause brake failure when it boils during hard braking.

Tyres go hard and crack with age, and from the ultraviolet rays in sunlight. This is particularly annoying if the tyres are expensive and have unworn treads, but it's inevitable.

Tyre problems

Tyres that have had the weight of the car on them in a single position for some time will develop flat spots, resulting in some (usually temporary) vibration. Old tyre walls may have cracks or (blister type) bulges, meaning new tyres are needed. All tyres should really be replaced after six or seven years, regardless of wear.

Shock absorbers (dampers)

With lack of use, the exposed central shafts can rust, then rip up the seals when next used.

Rubber and plastic

Radiator hoses harden, perish and split, resulting in total coolant loss. Gaiters/boots can crack. Wiper blades harden.

Electrics

GRP cars have earthing or grounding issues at the best of times, as plastic bodywork insulates rather than conducts electricity. Damp corrodes electrical connections, but cleaning and electrical grease help.

Batteries left flat for months will die – trickle chargers or solar chargers can prevent this. Wiring insulation can harden and fail, as can the copper strands within wires.

Exhaust systems

Exhaust gas contains water and corrosive compounds, so exhaust systems can corrode from the inside when the car is not used.

16 The Community

– key people, organisations & companies in the Cobra replica world

The Cobra Replica Club is an excellent introduction to the UK Cobra scene (www.cobraclub.com), You can either join the forum free by entering a name and password, or you can join the club properly, pay your £29 dues and get the club magazine, *Snake Torque*, sent to you. In the free forums you'll find some revealing chat, most of it constructive, and you'll get a good idea of the character of the replica marques.

In the USA, www.clubcobra.com is a useful and interesting club site/forum, and www.cobracountry.com is also good.

Some of the owners of the cars produced in larger numbers have formed clubs such as www.daxsportingclub.com, www.the289register.com, the Gardner Douglas Register (01622 851593), and in the USA www.ffrog.com supports Factory Five owners, of whom there are many.

The most obvious place to meet up with other Cobra enthusiasts is at kit car shows. These have become smaller in recent years because expensive automotive toys are products of boom times, but they're still fun.

Kitcar magazine's Stafford show in the UK offers a decent showing of Cobra replicas on the club stands, and chatting to owners gets you honest opinions about the cars they've built.

UK and USA kitcar clubs are listed in www.totalkitcar.com. It's well worth joining your local kit club as there will be somebody who can weld, somebody who can disentangle underdash tagliatelle and make lights work, and lots of others who can be replied upon to drink your beer and idle around in your garage supervising.

This car did not come with an enormous price tag, but it does look as through the owners are having enormous fun, doesn't it?

55

The smaller Cobra replica manufacturers are a tiny cottage industry and are very likely to become friends. Cobretti is one friendly bloke called Bob who builds a few very nice cars a year in a workshop at the bottom of his garden, and his customers usually become friends. AK also has a reputation for being thoroughly pleasant to deal with. The same applies in the US, but driving 3000 miles to visit your manufacturer is a problem, so the structure of the Cobra industry is different.

Sceniccartours (.com) runs tours to the 24 hour Le Mans race, which offers good value. The Cobra Club will also have people driving down for the race.

Gacé is a little hilltop town halfway from Calais to Le Mans, ideal for a lunchtime stop. The Bar du Centre does a nice steak frites. If stopped by cops, tell them you're Scottish (Ecossais), as French cops like the Scots.

Going to Le Mans, or anywhere else for that matter, in a Cobra replica with a crowd of other kit car drivers is thoroughly recommended. I used to organise a Le Mans camping trip for *Kitcar* magazine, which was excellent fun and attracted a good few Cobra replicas. There are many Le Mans trips you can join.

A V8 Cobra replica is absolutely ideal for French Route Nationale highways, now largely emptied by E-motorways. Bimble along at 60mph, elbow out, engine half asleep. Just avoid August, when holidaying French create traffic gridlocks to rival bank holiday A30 jams.

Trackday action is also strongly recommended, partly because it's enormous fun and partly for safety reasons: if you've pushed your car hard enough to spin it a few times on the track, you'll know when you're near the limit on the road as well. An insider tip is not to rush to get to a track day early, though – the queue to get on the track will thin out dramatically after lunch as everybody else gets tired. Take spare brake pads – if you're giving your car any real exercise you'll get through some. Re-tighten wheel nuts periodically during the day, as they work loose on the track.

Classic rallies of the lighter sort are excellent, and a '1968 Dax Tojeiro' although not in any sense a classic car, will be semi-eligible for some informal events. For serious classic rallying a Cobra replica wouldn't be anywhere near eligible, unless it were a Hawk 289 based on a single-donor MGB.

The kitcar show scene is good fun, too – there is normally camping during show weekends, and the cheerful company of plenty of other Cobra enthusiasts.

Vancouver's Jay Cavanagh runs an Everett-Morrison chassis with a Canadian Can-Am body and a huge big-block. Fuel prices in BC are about half those in the UK.

Factory Five occupies the same position in the US as Pilgrim does in the UK, having brought mass production methods to manufacturing kits. Both have sold a lot of cars.

There are currently four kitcar magazines serving kitcar and Cobra enthusiasts:
Kitcar
Complete Kit Car
TKC (produced by www.totalkitcar.com, a site which is well worth a surf for newcomers to the replica Cobra world)
Car Builder USA

17 Vital statistics
– essential data at your fingertips

Surfing the sites below will give you a very useful overview of the Cobra replica options and help you to identify what you will want from yours.

Four Dell 'Orto carbs on a hot Rover V8 give a Cobra a lot of power for its weight, and make the most fabulous noises. They stay fairly well in tune, too.

Don't discount an older Cobra: they simply don't wear out or rust. A Chevy 350 is just about run in at 100,000 miles, and a kit car chassis and body will last a lot longer than you will.

Cobra replicas UK

AK
www.aksports cars.com
Traditionally nice people. Good value cars, and they hold value. A solid, well-made and increasingly popular kit.

Ayrspeed (also in Canada, USA)
www.ayrspeed.com
The author's own concept: lightweight, single-donor Mazda Miata/MX5. 45+mpg, Japanese turbo power, serious handling. Cheap and cheerful, or expensive and nasty.

Cobretti Viper
www.cobrettiviperv8.com
Heavy construction, very good ride, wide front track gives excellent handling. Chevy preferred. Earlier four-cylinder Cobretti and Brightwheel Vipers suit Rover V8 upgrades.

Crendon CR427
www.crendonreplicas.com
One-man operation with high standards. Car aims to be a replica in spirit rather than a modernised lookalike.

Dax Tojeiro
www.daxcars.co.uk
The daddy of UK Cobra makers. Named after Ace/Cobra designer John Tojeiro. Still respected and carrying a premium when offered for sale.

Gardner Douglas
www.gdcars.com
Inspired by AC 289, but radically updated – backbone chassis and detachable stressed body are unique, with corrosion designed out. High engineering standards.

Hawk 289
www.hawkcars.co.uk

The auto shifter in my own previous Cobra replica knocked off value, but it had a ratchet shift and tuned autobox, making it either automatic or a clutchless three-speed manual – just like a dragster. Very fast or very lazy, according to mood. I'd have an auto every time.

With MGB axles and a 289/302 Ford, this is a spiritually authentic tribute to the exquisite AC 289, with high build quality. An AC Ace replica is also available.

Hawk 427/ Kirkham
www.hawkcars.co.uk
Imported by Hawk, alloy body, exquisite workmanship. Has also been sold by Shelby as CSX4000 series.

Parallel designs
www.paralleldesigns.co.uk
High-end Lamborghini replicator takes advantage of dirt-cheap BMW donors to enter the budget replica market.

Pilgrim Sumo (low budget)
www.pilgrimcars.com
Entry-level Cobra replica, bought and built in huge numbers for many years. Cheap and cheerful, good value.

Pilgrim Sumo (mid budget)
www.pilgrimcars.com
Many Pilgrims are now being built to a high standard with American V8s, and offer good value, although missing a premium badge.

Realm (previously Ram)
www.realmengineering.com
Previously made for the Bardahl one-make racing series. There was a four-wheel-drive Ram at one stage.

Superformance – see South Africa

Cobra replicas North America
Antique and Collectible
www.acautos.com
Comprehensive nut and bolt packs are a good sign. Long established company

making a variety of kits.

Backdraft – see South Africa

B & B Roadster
www.bandbroadster.com
Popular kit, customers' builds are usefully featured on website.

Classic Roadsters
www.classicroadsters.ca
Canadian company, eh. Optional leather trim and handling packages.

Classic Roadsters/Great Lakes replicas
www.sebring-mx.com
Longer wheelbase at 94in.

Cobray
www.cobrasnvettes.com
Uses a Corvette donor chassis – integrally tubbed body is 8in longer and 5in wider. Low-budget and suitable for the circumferentially challenged.

Cobrette
www.cobrareplicas.com
As above.

Emerson
www.beyondcobra.com
Ladder chassis, hand laid rather than chopper gun body. Body is 3in wider than standard, 4in longer, sits lower.

Era
www.erareplicas.com
Another established company. Visually accurate. Kit is supplied trial-assembled and on a returnable dolly.

Everett-Morrison
www.everett-morrison.com
Traditionally high quality. Wheelbase options include 90in, 96in, 98in.

Factory Five
www.factoryfive.com

7000 sold over 15 years – very well developed. Now in MkIV form. Available in the UK and Canada as well as USA.

Hunter
www.hunterscobrakits.com
Small company, making budget cars in 90in and 96in wheelbases with 3in dropped floor.

Hurricane
www.hurricane-motorsport.com
Concerned with accuracy. Company and customers are mutually supportive. 200-page build manual is a good sign.

JBL
www.jblmotor.com
Mid-front-engined semi-monocoque/ backbone road or race cars with custom inboard suspension. Technically impressive.

Kirkham (Shelby)
www.kirkhammotorsports.com
Aluminium-bodied 427 and 289, beautifully made in Polish aircraft factory with improved materials. Has also been available through Shelby with CSX numbers.

Lone Star Classics
www.lonestarclassics.com
20 years of experience, a 94in wheelbase, and they'll send a builder to help you assemble it in seven days.

Pacific Roadster
www.pacificroadster.com
Small, friendly company, aiming to offer good value for money.

Power Performance
www.pwrperformance.com
Round-tube ladder chassis, body with integral tub. Live, Jag or custom rear axle.

Premier Cobras

www.premiercobras.com
Original style round-tube frame and 427/428 big block is the recommended engine. Superleggera frame used to support GRP body.

Shelby– also see Kirkham and Superformance
www.shelbyautos.com

Shell Valley (Midstates)
www.shellvalley.com
Shell Valley has bought Midstates. It makes a wide range of replicas. Well established company.

Superformance – see South Africa

Unique
www.uniquemotorcars.com
Very well established. Available semi-assembled for easy build.

Westcoast
www.cobrakit.com

Company also sells erotic lingerie. Dramatically different Cobra replica: wide body, massive safety-inspired chassis.

Rest of the world
South Africa
Backdraft
www.backdraftracing.com (or .co.za)
Complete minus engine and box. Racing model also available. Exported from large South African factory.

Superformance
www.superformance.com
Complete minus engine and box. Have also been supplied as Shelby cars, and are Shelby licenced. Exported from substantial South African factory.

Australia
www.gforcesports cars.com
www.drbsports cars.com
www.cobrakits.com.au
www.classicrevival.com.au
www.python.com.au
www.cobtech.com.au

Germany
www.weineck-power.de
www.cobra427.de

The four top kitcar magazines: *Kitcar*, *TKC*, *Kit Car Builder*, and *Complete Kit Car*.

The Essential Buyer's Guide™ series ...

   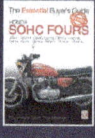 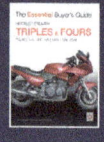  
    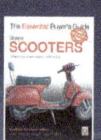  

... don't buy a vehicle until you've read one of these!

 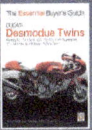 

£9.99-£12.99 / $19.95-$25.00
(prices subject to change, p&p extra).

For more details visit www.veloce.co.uk or email info@veloce.co.uk

Index

American Cobra replicas 5
Auctions 39-41

Brakes 4, 34
Bodywork 26, 27, 31, 32
Budgets 15, 16
Build or buy 15, 16, 48-50

Cabin size 7, 8
Chassis 3, 31, 33
Clubs 50, 55, 56
Costs 11
Controls 7
Compression test 30

Desirable/undesirable options 45-47

Electrics 36, 54
Engines 22, 29
Exhaust systems 14, 25, 54

Fuel systems 37

Gearboxes 22, 35, 36

Handling 4

Inspection equipment 20
Investment potential 10
Insurance 9, 30
Internet auctions 41
IVA test 17, 27-29, 44

Key inspection points 23-25, 38

Lack of use problems 53, 54
Luggage space 8, 13

Manufacturers UK 58, 59
Manufacturers USA/worldwide 59-61

Original Cobras 3, 4

Paint problems 51, 52
Paperwork 18, 19, 21, 27-29, 42-44
Parts issues 9, 12
Payment options 19, 37
Professional/MoT inspection 19, 38

Road fund licence 19, 42, 44

Service history 42, 44
Servicing costs 12
Suspension 33-35

Track days 57
Turbocharging 16
Tyres and wheels 32, 33, 54

Unleaded fuel 29

Values 9, 11, 45-47

Weather protection 14